T0110873

BLOOD AND FIRE

The Redemptive Story of Cain & the God of Compassion

Dr. Victor T. Nyarko

authorHOUSE®

AuthorHouse™
1663 Liberty Drive
Bloomington, IN 47403
www.authorhouse.com
Phone: 833-262-8899

Published by AuthorHouse 11/28/2020

ISBN: 978-1-6655-0726-4 (sc)
ISBN: 978-1-6655-0725-7 (e)

Library of Congress Control Number: 2020922279

Print information available on the last page.

Scriptures are taken from the King James Version of the Bible.

This book is printed on acid-free paper.

PRESENTED TO

FROM

DATE

Other Exciting Books by the Author.

DIVINE EMPOWERMENT

This book is an exposition on the power of the efficacious blood of Jesus Christ, the legacy and empowerment it provided for the first Apostles, for today's believer in Jesus Christ and for all who will come after. It reveals the resources that God through Christ has made available and at our disposal for the successful accomplishment of the great commission. It also teaches the reader, how one can tap into these resources by believing it, claiming it and possessing it.

ISBN97

A DISCONNECTED GENERATION

This book presents striking differences between the generation of Moses and the generation of Joshua. Although Joshua's génération witnessed a glimpse of the miracles and wonder workings of God, they lacked a personal relationship with the God of their fathers and the God of Israel.

ISBN 1-59330-075-1

DEALING WITH REJECTION

Rejection of one kind or another is inevitable throughout ones' life; therefore any tool that can be acquired to help deal with it should be a welcome choice. In this book, Dr. Nyarko presents the key elements that lead to the feeling of rejection and how to deal with rejection from a biblical perspective.

ISBN1-59330-471-4

BEAUTY FOR ASHES

It has been the church's tradition to think that great revival could be sparked by extensive advertising, putting up the right preacher and playing the right music. If these are true ingredients for revival, then John the Baptist' revival which ignited and blazed a trail in the desolate and obscure wilderness of Judea wouldn't have had the impact it did. On the contrary, out of the ashes of repentance comes revival, refreshing restitution and restoration.

ISBN 1-59330-605-9

WHERE ARE THE FATHERS

The lack of fathers at home has been one of society's greatest dilemmas of our time. This book has a timely word from the Lord for everyone. God our father is calling all fathers through the pen of this godly author and father, back to the honorable and critical role of fatherhood. Get ready, read it, repent and pass it on. **ISBN13:9781593302436**

KINGDOM WORSHIP

Music is part of worship but good music alone does not constitute worship. In this book, the various Hebrew words for 'praise' are described. It sheds light on the true meaning of worship and what the popular command 'Hallelujah' means in the praise and worship of God. It comes from two Hebrew words *Halal* which is the most radical form of praise and *Yah* which is the short form for Jehovah. To worship God, goes far beyond being an act. It should be a personal encounter with God's presence which should lead to the worshipper, leaving His presence with fulfillment and gratification. In brief, this book focuses on what it means to halal (praise) God, who ought to Halal (praise) Him and where he ought to be Halal (praised). **ISBN 978-1-4984-3509-3**

THE PRODIGAL FATHER

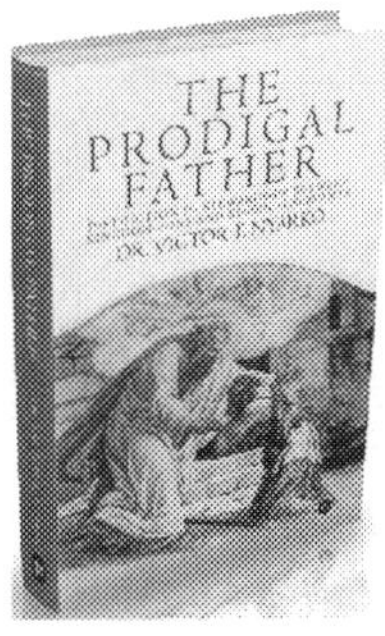

What has become popularly but also erroneously referred to as the story of the 'prodigal son' is part of a larger revelation that Jesus wanted to show his church. This book then culminates with the distinction that our Lord Jesus makes between Sonship and servanthood in his vineyard parable about the servants and sons who were sent out by the Lord to work on his vineyard. Are all humanity Sons of God through procreation as many claim? Or, is there a distinction between Kingdom-Sons and Kingdom-Servants of God? This book's approach to the story will leave you amused, instructed, enlightened, stirred up, and challenged, but definitely not bored! **ISBN: 978-1-947349-23-0**

THE ORDER OF MELCHIZEDEK

This book takes the reader on an intriguing and interesting journey into the life and person, of a strange and isolated but unique bible personage called Melchizedek, He appears momentarily on the scene of bible history with the great Patriarch Abraham and then disappears from the pages of history just as suddenly as he appeared. All other references in the bible about him is traced back to this one occasion. He is said to be without father, mother, nor descent, having neither beginning of days, nor end of life. So the questions then is; who was Melchizedek? In what ways does his priestly order align with the Lord Jesus and yet differs from the Aaronic order of Priesthood? Why should Melchizedek, and he alone, of all the Old Testament

characters be thought of in a way that defies human mortality? This book's approach to the life and person of Melchizedek will leave you amused, instructed, enlightened, stirred up, and challenged, but definitely not bored!
ISBN: 978-1-947349-21-6

THE 4 DEGREES OF RELATIONSHIP

It's a matter of common knowledge that many of the headaches one goes through in life are as a result of bad associations. This book is about relationships, friendships and associations, which is one of the key areas of our lives that we need to safeguard against. The key goal of this book is to teach the reader how to model their sphere of relationship after the pattern of Christ. We all, to some degree, have a sphere of association with other people who have the potential to impact the way we behave and the decisions we make in life. As the say goes, "no man is an Island," because we are all interconnected in one way or the other. That is why as humans, and by instinct people will put their lives in danger to save even strangers whom they do not know or have ever met.

One cannot underestimate the importance that Jesus placed on his associations because it is out of his associations that he chose the 12 disciples who he would later refer to as his friends. It was also out of the 12 disciples that he later chose the 3 disciples (Peter, James and John) who became his inner circle and confidants. **ISBN: 9781642371093**
eISBN: 9781642371086

ANTIDOTE;
HOW THE BLOOD OF THE LAMB GOES TO WORK FOR THE SINS OF HUMANITY

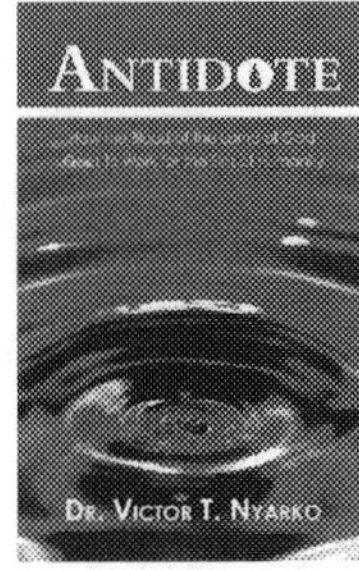

It was D.L. Devan who said; "The subject of the blood of the lamb of God and the mystery surrounding this subject, will ever remain one of the richest gold mines of evangelical thought. It occupies a central position in the doctrine of atonement, just like the phrase 'God is Spirit' occupies in relation to the doctrine of God." There is literally no Sunday that one would leave an Apostolic or Pentecostal church service without hearing the mention of the blood in one way or the other. At times through sermons, or in prayers, in exhortations or some other manner. Even casual, everyday conversations among born-again Believers, often triggers the usage or reference to the blood of Jesus. Either by claiming something by faith through the blood, by rebuking the works and schemes of our common adversary and enemy of our soul through the blood or by rejoicing for victories won through the blood of Jesus.

In this book I will expound on what makes the blood of the lamb of God precious and unique. Also, how the blood of the Lamb of God goes to work on behalf of the Believer or born-again Christian as well as sinners seeking salvation and deliverance from the yoke and bondage of sin and spiritual death so that the next time you sing the popular chorus; "there is power, power, wonder working power in the blood of the lamb..." you will exactly understand the principle behind how the power in the blood of the Lamb is put to work.

ISBN: 978-1-5462-7296-0

DEDICATION

This book is dedicated to the Purity Movement.

To
All the young men and women in Victory Family Worship Center and other churches who have set themselves aside to live pure in a polluted world.

May the Lord be your strength and guide
as you continue to let your lives shine
bright in the dark world around you.

To
Joan Elaine my wife, life-long companion
and my best friend and our children and
greatest admirers, Tori, Joash and Vanya.

CONTENTS

ACKNOWLEDGEMENT

Many thanks to the following people for your selfless service in making this book a possibility.

Editorial staff:
Felicia Amma Antwi (Ghana),

Photography:
Victoria Nyarko (VFWC)

Cover Design:
Publisher

CHAPTER ONE

INTRODUCTION

Many people have the tendency to either want to ignore one piece of scripture to establish another in an attempt to expound scripture. At other times, they try to condemn a portion of scripture to develop another part of scripture. There is, however, such a beautiful harmony in the word of God. If one comes to a clear understanding and revelation of God's word, one would not have to take that conflicting approach to interpret the holy scriptures. In my years of pulpit ministry, I have noticed that when some preach about Bible characters who had deep flaws in their walk with God, they always stop at their sins, their shortcomings, and the consequences or punishment they may have endured result of their failures. Still, I have found out on the contrary that God does not stop at where men fail. The merciful God always goes beyond man's inability and continues until the miraculous work of redemption is entirely wrought.

This is because Christ came to die for the pitfalls of man because of grace. Grace is a redemption story because there is no redemption without the act of grace or mercy being shown first. I can give countless examples in the Bible, like Cain, Miriam, Moses, Jacob, Saul, and many others who, despite their failures, later became the pillars of the Judeo-Christian faith and values.

Among these examples are the likes of:

1. Moses and Miriam had good intentions and began their walk of faith with God on excellent and substantial grounds; however, they nearly ended up forfeiting all they had worked for - except that God, in His abundance of grace and love, showed them mercy.
2. Others like Saul later became Paul upon conversion, Jacob, and Cain, just to name a few.

One would notice that although they did not start well and also messed up really bad. Still, as always, God brought great redemption their way, and they ended up becoming pillars of the faith in their day.

In this book, I will be delving into the story of Cain and Abel, the first products of human procreation through Adam and Eve. This story is unique because there are a couple of things done that were unknown to human history. It is a story that began with God's wrath against sinful human nature. Yet it ended with a decisive act of redemption that comes from a repentant heart of a sinner and the forgiving Spirit of the merciful God of Heaven and of all creation.

Above all, the story of Cain and Abel's sacrifices made unto God served as a principle that would, later on, be followed by servants of God throughout dispensations.

It is worth mentioning that contrary to what I was taught in Sunday school as a child, Cain and Abel's story takes a lot of twists and turns that will excite the reader's imagination. It will also impact the reader by knowing some essential spiritual principles that transcend time, people and space.

Buckle your seat belt and join me on this intriguing journey into the world of humanity's first family. It promises to be a reading that you will never forget. It comes with life lessons that will enrich, empower, and leave indelible marks on your spiritual life for good.

CHAPTER TWO

ATTITUDE IS EVERYTHING

Let us first consider one of the critical passages of scripture that will serve as our context for this book before moving on to the actual text.

Our Context; Matt 3:1-12

1] *In those days came John the Baptist, preaching in the wilderness of Judaea,*

2] *And saying, Repent ye: for the kingdom of heaven is at hand.*

3] *For this is he that was spoken of by the Prophet Esaias, saying, the voice of one crying in the wilderness, prepare ye the way of the Lord, make his paths straight.*

4] *And the same John had his raiment of camel's hair, and a leathern girdle about his loins; and his meat was locusts and wild honey.*

5] *Then went out to him Jerusalem, and all Judaea, and all the region round about Jordan,*

6] *And were baptized of him in Jordan, confessing their sins.*

7] *But when he saw many of the Pharisees and Sadducees come to his baptism, he said unto them, O generation of vipers, who hath warned you to flee from the wrath to come?*
8] *Bring forth therefore fruits meet for repentance:*
9] *And think not to say within yourselves, we have Abraham to our father: for I say unto you, that God is able of these stones to raise up children unto Abraham.*
10] *And now also the ax is laid unto the root of the trees: therefore every tree which brunet not forth good fruit is hewn down, and cast into the fire.*
11] *I indeed baptize you with water unto repentance: but he that cometh after me is mightier than I, whose shoes I am not worthy to bear: he shall baptize you with the Holy Ghost, and with fire:*
12] *Whose fan is in his hand, and he will thoroughly purge his floor, and gather his wheat into the garner; but he will burn up the chaff with unquenchable fire.*

Throughout the Bible, many things have been used as symbols of The Holy Spirit. For example, at times, oil is used as a symbol of the Holy Spirit. In other instances, the rain has also been used for the same purpose. However, I would like to dwell on fire as a symbol of the Holy Spirit for this book's purpose. John the Baptizer, baptized with water, but he was the same one who also bore witness that someone is coming after he leaves the scene, who will baptize with the Holy Ghost and fire. So, what is the significance of this fire referred to by John? What does the fire do in the life of the Believer? These are questions that I will be tackling in this book in later chapters.

John the Baptist says: "***He will baptize you with the Holy Ghost and fire, whose fan is in His hand. He will thoroughly purge His floor and gather His wheat into the garner, but He will burn up the chaff with unquenchable fire.***"

By the above statement, John meant that neither the ***wheat*** nor the ***chaff*** will be lost during the final sorting of souls that can and will be done by God only. This is because none shall be able to escape from His hands, and none shall escape the wrath of God. To better expound on this statement, I would like to consider it from the cultural background of olden Palestine times. During that era of human history, it was typical for every wheat farmer to have a threshing floor. After the harvest, the Farmer would usually have an ox that will walk around upon the wheat on the floor to tread out the grain from the ears of grain. The threshing floor would usually be in the open, having no roof to it. It would often be a flat rock. That is the illustration that John was using as a backdrop for the scripture above.

However, the contrast is that the Farmer's goal and focus are mainly the wheat rather than the chaff that the grain leaves behind. God, on the other hand, is interested in both the grain and the chaff. God is interested in both the righteous and the wicked, except that God has different rewards and eternal destinations for each of them.

Now, let's move further to the scriptural passage that will serve as the book's primary Bible text. This could be found in the fourth chapter of the book of Genesis.

Genesis 4:1-17

And Adam knew Eve, his wife, and she conceived, and bare Cain, and said, I have gotten a man from the LORD.

2 *And she again bare his brother Abel. And Abel was a keeper of sheep, but Cain was a tiller of the ground.*
3 *And in process of time it came to pass, that Cain brought of the fruit of the ground an offering unto the LORD.*
4 *And Abel, he also brought of the firstlings of his flock and of the fat thereof. And the LORD had respect unto Abel and to his offering:*
5 *But unto Cain and to his offering he had not respect. And Cain was very wroth, and his countenance fell.*
6 *And the LORD said unto Cain, Why art thou wroth? and why is thy countenance fallen?*
7 *If thou doest well, shalt thou not be accepted? and if thou doest not well, sin lieth at the door. And unto thee shall be his desire, and thou shalt rule over him.*
8 *And Cain talked with Abel his brother: and it came to pass, when they were in the field, that Cain rose up against Abel his brother, and slew him.*
9 *And the LORD said unto Cain, Where is Abel thy brother? And he said, I know not: Am I my brother's keeper?*
10 *And he said, What hast thou done? the voice of thy brother's blood crieth unto me from the ground.*
11 *And now art thou cursed from the earth, which hath opened her mouth to receive thy brother's blood from thy hand;*
12 *When thou tillest the ground, it shall not henceforth yield unto thee her strength; a fugitive and a vagabond shalt thou be in the earth.*

13 *And Cain said unto the LORD, My punishment is greater than I can bear.*
14 *Behold, thou hast driven me out this day from the face of the earth; and from thy face shall I be hid; and I shall be a fugitive and a vagabond in the earth; and it shall come to pass, that every one that findeth me shall slay me.*
15 *And the LORD said unto him, Therefore whosoever slayeth Cain, vengeance shall be taken on him sevenfold. And the LORD set a mark upon Cain, lest any finding him should kill him.*
16 *And Cain went out from the presence of the LORD, and dwelt in the land of Nod, on the east of Eden.*
17 *And Cain knew his wife; and she conceived, and bare Enoch: and he builded a city, and called the name of the city, after the name of his son, Enoch.*

A critical look into the book of Genesis will reveal the following synopsis about the story of creation;

Genesis **Chapter 1:** reveals the magnificent story of creation, which also marks the beginning of all things both in the heavens and on the earth. This beautiful beginning encompasses all flora and fauna worlds that inhabit terrestrial, airborne, and aquatic worlds. It includes both the microscopic, macroscopic and the seen and unseen all existing alongside each other.

Genesis Chapter 2: reveals authority given by God the Creator to creation under lords, which is the man and which are Adam and Eve.

Genesis Chapter 3: reveals the fall of man and the consequences that followed as a result of the fall.

Genesis Chapter 4: reveals the remedy to the fall of man. That remedy, which will later be discussed in detail as being Blood and Fire, forms the basis of the divine principles introduced and expounded in this book.

After the Lord had ousted Adam and Eve from the Garden of Eden, Adam knew his wife (Eve), and she conceived and gave birth to Cain and Abel. Since there was only one conception, we can therefore conclude that Cain and Abel were twins.

The above text in Genesis chapter 4 reveals that Abel was a keeper of sheep, and his brother Cain was a tiller of the ground. This is important because it represents the two primary forms of farming: animal husbandry and crop husbandry.

Husbandry, by definition, refers to the cultivation and breeding of both crops and animals. (Dictionary.com)

It is worth noting that neither could stand on its own because each needs the other. Hence there has always been a symbiotic association between these two types of farming. The animals need the grass or feed cultivated on the land to live. The earth also needs the animals' droppings to build the necessary nutrients that the soil requires to be productive.

With this fact established, it is therefore appropriate that the two brothers will each pursue one form of farming as their means of sustenance. Thus, Cain was right in tilling the ground, for God had said to Adam, in Genesis 3:19), ***"In the sweat of your face thou shalt eat bread."***

If that be the case, then it means that someone has got to till the land and so Cain was right in choosing to be a tiller of the ground.

It also implies that Abel was also right in his choice since each form of farming thrives on the other's existence. However, in the process of time when Abel offered the firstlings of his flock unto the Lord as a sacrifice, the Bible says; God "*had respect*" of Abel's offering. The Lord was pleased with Abel's sacrifice because it was a complete offering with blood. This was a picture of the ultimate gift of the precious blood of Jesus, the Lamb of God. This was also the third time the blood of innocence was shed; the first time, with Adam, was when his side was opened to bring forth the rib to bring forth Adam's bride. The second time was when God sacrificed an innocent animal for the covering of Adam and Eve. The third time, Abel made the burnt offering to the Lord of the innocent firstling of his flock. This is because the animal's age to be offered had to be in the innocent years of its life. Notice that in the garden of Eden, when man fell to sin, God sacrificed an innocent animal for the covering of Adam and Eve while they were in their rebellious state of sin. This is the same incredible love and grace that God has demonstrated towards humanity from generation to generation.

Romans 5:8-9, ***"But God commendeth his love towards us, in that, while we were yet sinners, Christ died for us. Much more then, being now justified by his blood, we shall be saved from wrath through him"***

However, when Cain brought his offering, God "did not show respect and acceptance." Ladies and gentlemen, brothers and sisters, there is a big problem here because, as established a few paragraphs earlier, both crop farming and animal husbandry were necessary. They were both needed to sustain human life and the growth of crops, so why would God accept one and refuse the other?

I want to help you to understand why the acceptance of one sacrifice over the other. But before I get deeper into that, I want you to toss aside the prejudices most people have learned concerning individual interpretations of scripture and which has been accepted as scriptural truth. Cain was right in tilling the ground because God ordained that it has to be done, and someone had to do it, which happened to be Cain. Abel was also right in rearing sheep because it was ordained by God as well. Therefore, Abel and Cain were right in their choice of husbandry. The big question then is, why did God reject Cain's offering but accepted that of Abel? Is it because of the differences in the type of substance they offered, or is it because of some other reason?

Many years ago as a child growing up in Church, my beloved Sunday school teacher taught me that Abel's sacrifice was accepted by God because he offered to God the best of the firstling among his flock while Cain on the other hand offered unto the Lord some rotten tomatoes, rotten garden eggs or rotten farm produce of some sort.

Could you believe that this interpretation stayed with me for many years even into my adult life? Although it was not the truth of scripture because the Bible never made mention of any rotten tomatoes, rotten garden eggs, or any awful farm produce in the account given in the Bible. I believe the story was twisted in good faith by my Sunday school teacher in an attempt to bring to the understanding of our little minds what may have been the cause for the rejection of Cain's sacrifice. However, despite the motive for that sort of interpretation, and the fact that it may have been deliberately done in good faith, the damage it caused to my understanding and that of the other Sunday school children in my class, lasted for decades into my adult life.

My advice to teachers is to teach our Sunday school children precisely what is written in the Bible and leave the rest for the Spirit of the Lord to shed light on their understanding. Desist from sharing an erroneous version of a Bible story with the hope that our children will eventually come to a better understanding of the full knowledge of the truth when they become adults.

Two Types of Altars

Scripture teaches us of basically two types of altars, namely: righteous and evil altars. The first time that a distinction of these two altars were made is in the fourth chapter of the book of Genesis when the two sons of Adam, namely Cain, and Abel decided to build altars upon which to offer their sacrifices unto the Lord. According to Scripture, Cain brought to the altar, an offering of the fruit of the ground. Cain, who was a crop farmer, placed vegetables on his altar. On the other hand, Abel brought of the firstborn of his flock and of the fat portions because he reared livestock. Notice that God's reaction to the two offerings on the two altars was totally different. God openly rejected Cain's offering, while He demonstrated acceptance of Abel's sacrificial offering.

Why did God reject Cain's offering?

1) The first reason that I will give to this question is because in Genesis 3;17, it's stated that God had already cursed the ground.

Genesis 3:17, "*And to Adam He said, Because you have listened and given heed to the voice of your wife and have eaten of the tree of which I commanded you, saying, You shall not eat of it, the ground is under a curse because of you; in sorrow and toil shall you eat [of the fruits] of it all the days of your life.*"

The point here is that, how can God use the fruit of the "accursed" to redeem the soul of the man offering it?. That therefore explains why God had no pleasure in Cain's sacrifice. It is obvious and I am certain that Adam at some point in time, may have made his two sons aware of the fact that God had cursed the ground because of the sins of Adam and his wife Eve. It is also very likely that Adam may have also informed his two sons of God's act of redemption by shedding blood through the killing of a lamb and using the skin or fur of the lamb as a covering for their nakedness. That being the case, why would Cain insist in bringing to God an offering from something that has already been cursed? How could he secure atonement for his soul using an accursed thing?

The bigger question that one needs to ask is that, if indeed Cain was warned by his father that the ground is cursed, then why did he still went ahead and do it? We will come to understand later in this chapter and book that Cain was driven by the spirit of rebellion, arrogance, and the desire to do things his own way. A lesson that we can learn from God's reaction to Cain's offering is that God is very selective of what's given to Him at a righteous altar as well as the manner in which it is presented. This separates the Almighty God from idols (demon-gods) who on the other hand, are so desperate to be worship that they will accept any accursed thing offered to them by their human attendants.

Idols are so desperate for expression in the world of men that they will accept any offering, sacrifice, act of worship regardless of how it is offered, provided they can gain access to mankind. God on the other hand is sovereign, holy, and separate from sin and therefore He is particular on what He accepts as offering. Meaning that God cannot be manipulated by what we offer to Him at His holy altar. It is also worth noting that God accepted Abel's sacrifice on the altar because Abel gave God exactly what God required for the remission of sins of the soul of man – the blood of an innocent animal, from the best of his flock. This I believe he learnt from what his father may have told them about how God covered their parent's nakedness through the slaughtering of a lamb and the use of the lamb's skin as covering.

Cain therefore became the biblical example as well as symbol for an evil and defiled altar while his brother became an example of what a righteous altar is. Cain's altar was built on evil, pride, defiance, rebellion, rage, jealousy, selfish ambition, and murder. The god behind Cain's evil altar was the "idol of self ", self-will and, ultimately, Satan who is also the father of all that stands against God. This is why Cain could not resist arguing with God. The Bible says about Cain:

> *"And the Lord said to Cain, 'Where is Abel your brother?' And he said, 'I do not know. Am I my brother's keeper?"*

What an act of arrogance Cain displayed in his response to God. Who talks to God with such arrogance, disrespect, and pride as if they are equal with God.

It is worth noting that Cain's offering was rejected by God not because of the kind of substance it is comprised of, but rather because of the Spirit in which it was given or offered unto the Lord. This conclusion can easily be inferred from the question that God posed to Cain after he was angry because of the rejection of his offering. The question God posed to Cain makes it very clear that the denial of his offering had nothing to do with the nature of the substance that was offered. Instead had to do with the Spirit in which it was given. God said to Cain ***"If thou doest well, shalt thou not be accepted?" (*** Genesis 4:7)

This is not a question about the nature of the substance offered. This is an attitude problem. It was a question aimed at addressing the attitude of Cain rather than the type of material he offered unto God. In other words, God was saying to Cain; "I will accept your offering if you will change your attitude and do well. However, if you don't then sin is crouching at your door like an angry lion, waiting to pounce on you and devour you if you don't have a change of heart."

God was indicating to Cain that he had an attitude problem because he was jealous of his brother Abel and of his brother's offering. The lesson that God was trying to teach Cain here is that; "it was not the offering that God wanted, but rather, it is Cain himself that God was interested in. On many occasions when Believers approach God, we focus on the substance of our offering instead of the condition of our heart but God is interested in the condition of our heart than the physical material we approach Him with. God was saying to Cain, *"I'm glad to accept the offering when you bring it to me with a pure heart and without bitterness, jealousy, and resentment against your brother"*. When you approach God with sin in your heart against your brother, the offering you lay before God means nothing to God. As a matter of fact, the Bible describes the odor of such offering as stinking before God. God was trying to teach Cain, the same lesson that God has been trying to teach each and every one of his children in their walk with the Lord. And that lesson is simple and still the same as God said to King Saul in his disobedience towards Him; *"to obey is better than sacrifice"*.

Isn't this precisely the same spiritual principle that Jesus was trying to teach when He said;

> ***"When thou bringest thy gift before the altar and your brother has ought against you, go and put the matter right with your***

> ***brother. Then come and offer thy gift"* (Matthew 5:23-24).**

Let's be real and straight forward about this. It's precisely the same principle that Jesus was teaching when He made that utterance in Matthew chapter five. God accepted Abel's offering and reject Cain's, offering because Abel's offering was provided from a pure heart, and Cain's wasn't. Thank God that the acceptance or rejection has nothing to do with the nature of substance but rather it is based on the condition of the heart. This spiritual principle, as simple as it may seem, holds the key to the reason why many prayers of the saints of God go unanswered. Before God, the condition of our heart is paramount to whether the lip services we offered unto God in worship and praises will be acceptable to God or not. When was the last time you conducted a 'litmus test' of the spiritual condition your heart before the Lord? When was the last time you made a request to God simply because you were envious of your brother or sister's blessings or something that they had and you did not have? When was the last time you were unhappy and could not rejoice with another brother or sister because they seem to be getting ahead at a very fast pace and making better progress in their lives than you have been making? When was the last time you took a pause just to examine the condition of your heart before God? As simple and straightforward as this may seem, that is what led to the rejection of Cain's offering, and the same could lead to the rejection of your offering and mine if we are not careful to always address the condition of our hearts before God.

Let's take a more in-depth look into the condition of Cain's heart and his attitude which later resulted in the apparent consequences of his wicked heart. Cain, after being warned by God, refused to choose the right path and to proceed in the right direction. Instead, his evil and envious heart led him to murder his brother and when questioned by God of the whereabouts of his brother, he tried to conceal it. He had the nerve to answer back to God by asking God in response to God's question to him. Cain's killing of his brother, Abel, gives us a picture of the killing of Jesus by His own brethren and countrymen.

Notice that Cain was not just envious and angry at his brother. His words and actions depicted that he was also mad at God. Take a look at his response to God after he slew his brother, and God asked him about where his brother was. Cain responded and said to God, "***Am I my brother's keeper***? It is interesting to note that this is a question that Cain would later on in his life have to answer for himself. However, that would be after he has learned his lesson the hard way, that indeed each of us is our brother's or sister's keeper.

One of the most common and most prevailing internal problems in most Churches today is people's attitudes.

In conclusion, I decided to give this chapter the title: 'Attitude Is Everything' because attitude is one of the subject areas that are the least addressed from the pulpit these days. One of the most common and most prevailing internal problems in most of our Churches today has to do with the attitude of people. As one who has been pastoring for several years now, I can tell you that, lousy conduct is everywhere in the body of Christ now and it is one of the leading problems that Pastors have to deal with more often than any other issue in the Church. In our Churches today, one will find born-again believers with very distasteful and disrespectful attitudes towards their leaders as well as towards their fellow brothers and sisters in the congregation. I was once told that upon being cautioned by a Pastor about the potential of a trip and fall hazard as a result of some congregants' habit of charging their cell phones on the electrical power outlets along the hallways and passage in the sanctuary, one congregation member responded by telling her Pastor that she pays her tithes and gives offering so she has the right to use electrical power outlets in the Church. That was beside the point the Pastor wanted to make since the Pastor was more concerned about the possibility of someone tripping over and falling as a result of phone charging cords rather than the amount of electricity the charging of the phone would incur.

In our day and age, a Church can be seriously sued for damages caused by any injury that occurs within the confinement of a Church facility. Besides, not all who visit Church on Sundays are people of the faith hence I believe the Pastor was looking out to prevent any such accident or incident rather than save on the Church's electricity bill.

These days, we have thrown out of the Church, respect, and decency towards elders. Instead, the display of rudeness and bad attitude is gradually creeping its ugly head into the Church of Jesus Christ and among many congregations. These days, the attitudes of many Believers simply undermine their profession of faith because as the saying goes; "our actions speak louder than our words". We may openly and loudly confess our love for God, but if our actions do not back the confession of our love for God, then our faith is vain.

CHAPTER THREE

THE THREE DEADLY ERRORS TO AVOID AT ALL COST

It is worth noting that in **2 Peter 2:15,** where some of the darkest passages in the Old Testament history are revisited by Peter in the New Testament. While Peter refers only to a single instance that had to do with the mischievous ways of Balaam and Peter calls them *'accursed children'*. Jude on the other hand takes it further in **Jude 1:11**, and introduces three of these darkest passages of the Old Testament by mentioning in addition to Balaam, the errors of Cain and Kora.

Beside besides the original story's narratives in Genesis's book about the two brothers Cain and Abel, there are only three other scriptural references to Cain in the entire Bible. However, it is worth noting that every one of the other three scriptures describes Cain in a very hostile and unfavorable manner due to his actions.

Hebrews 11:4

> ***4 By faith Abel offered unto God a more excellent sacrifice than Cain, by which he obtained witness that he was righteous, God testifying of his gifts: and by it he being dead yet speaketh.***

I John 3;10-12

> ***10 In this the children of God are manifest, and the children of the devil: whosoever doeth not righteousness is not of God, neither he that loveth not his brother.***
> ***11 For this is the message that ye heard from the beginning, that we should love one another.***
> **12** *Not as Cain, who was of that wicked one, and slew his brother.* ***And wherefore slew he him? Because his own works were evil, and his brother's righteous.***

Jude 1:11

> ***"Woe unto them! For they have gone in the way (method) of Cain, and ran greedily after the error of Balaam for reward, and perished in the gainsaying of Core."***

This is because when men deviate from God's holy ordinances, there are basically three ways by which evil men orchestrate their evil intentions.

1) *The way (method) of Cain,*
2) *The error of Balaam,*
3) *The gainsaying of Korah.*

None is better than the other because they are three examples of similar wickedness and ungodliness, they are all condemned by the word of God and they all lead to the same end result. Cain, like the inhabitants of Sodom and Gomorrha, outraged the laws of nature. Balaam, like the impure angels, despised the sovereignty of God. Korah, like those who disbelieved the report of the spies, spoke evil of dignities. Jude foretells their destruction, because they proclaim Cain's shameless malice, Balaam's filthy covetousness, and Kora's seditious and ambitious head. Jude therefore concluded by pronouncing 'woes' and judgement upon people who orchestrate these three errors in the body of Christ. Wickedness has its end in woes and the end of woes is usually death. However, woes do not come without warning. As an example, God foretells the ruin that it may be averted, as in the notable case of the Ninevites where the Prophet Jonah was sent as a messenger to sound a warning.

Notice also that the most fearful woes are those which are spiritual in their nature hence as Ministers of the Lord, we ought to teach the church the terror of going against God's Law as well as the blessedness of following his ordinances and reaping its many promises. In the case of Cain, Balaam and Korah; there is a threefold variety in godless transgression. There is an outrage against the laws of nature. «For they went in the way of Cain. That was a way of hypocrisy of envy, of selfishness, hatred, violence and cruelty. Look at the seriousness of the consequences of these 3 errors according to Jude, as recorded in **Jude 1;12-13**

> **"12** ***These are spots in your feasts of charity, (referring to the 3 errors) when they feast with you, feeding themselves without fear: clouds they are without water, carried about of winds; trees whose fruit withereth, without fruit, twice dead, plucked up by the roots;***
> ***13 Raging waves of the sea, foaming out their own shame; wandering stars, to whom is reserved the blackness of darkness for ever.***

1) THE WAY OF CAIN

Scripture teaches that there are basically two types of altars, namely: righteous and evil altars. The first time that a distinction of these two altars were made is in the fourth chapter of the book of Genesis when the two sons of Adam, namely Cain, and Abel decided to build altars upon which to offer their sacrifices unto the Lord.

According to Scripture, Cain brought to the altar, an offering of the fruit of the ground. Cain, who was a crop farmer, placed vegetables on his altar. On the other hand, Abel brought of the firstborn of his flock and of the fat portions because he reared livestock. Notice that God's did not hide His pleasure and acceptance of Abel's offering and neither did God hide His displeasure of Cain's offering from God's reaction to the two offerings on the two altars.

God openly rejected Cain's offering, while He

demonstrated acceptance of Abel's sacrificial offering. Cain then went on to become the first great criminal; the first to outrage the laws of nature.

Why did God reject Cain's offering?

1) The first reason that I will give to this question is because in Genesis 3;17, it's stated that God had already cursed the ground.

Genesis 3:17, *"And to Adam He said, Because you have listened and given heed to the voice of your wife and have eaten of the tree of which I commanded you, saying, You shall not eat of it,* ***the ground is under a curse because of you****; in sorrow and toil shall you eat [of the fruits] of it all the days of your life."*

The point here is that, the reason for his offering was for the redemption of his soul but how can a Holy God use the fruit of the "***accursed***" to redeem the soul of the man offering it? That therefore explains why God had no pleasure in Cain's sacrifice.

It is obvious and certain that Adam may have already communicated to his two sons the fact that God had cursed the ground because of his sin. Adam may have done that especially so Cain since he chose that line of trade that had to do with tilling the earth for the produce of the ground. It is also worth noting that God accepted Abel's sacrifice on the altar because Abel gave God exactly what He required for the remission of sins of the soul of man – the blood of an innocent animal, from the best of his flock! Why - because Adam may have given the two boys a hint, that when your Mom and I sinned against God; God sheared blood by slaughtering a lamb and using its skin to cloth our nakedness. Just like Adam may have told them about the cursed ground. That being the case, why would Cain insist in bringing to God an offering from something that had already been cursed? How could he secure atonement for his soul using an accursed thing?

The bigger question that one needs to ask is that, if indeed Cain was warned by his father that the ground is cursed, then why did he still went ahead and do it? I will show you in a moment because that's the same error and spirit that is seen in churches and among believers today. Cain was driven by the spirit of rebellion, arrogance, and the desire to do things his own way. This spirit of rebellion is one of the three errors that the Beloved Apostle and brother of Jesus by name Jude was referring to as the "way of Cain" in the eleventh verse of his epistle. Cain therefore became the biblical example as well as symbol for an evil and defiled altar while his brother became an example of what a righteous altar is. This is because Cain's altar was built on evil, pride, defiance, rebellion, rage, jealousy, selfish ambition, and murder. The god behind Cain's evil altar was the "idol of self ", self-will and, ultimately, Satan who is also the father of all that stands against God. This is why Cain could not resist arguing with God. This is the Libertine spirit we are seeing today. Government want to interfere with the way we raise our children so they want to pull away parental control and;

1) teaching our little kindergarten kids that you can be whatever you feel like being boy or girl even if you were not created as one by birth.
2) teaching teenage girls that you can abort your baby without your parents knowing it.

Libertinism: according to dictionary.com is defined as;

> ***"A libertine is one devoid of most moral principles, a sense of responsibility, or sexual restraints, which are seen as unnecessary or undesirable, especially one who ignores or even spurns accepted morals and forms of behavior sanctified by the larger society. Libertinism is described as an extreme form of hedonism."***

They follow the ways of Cain by murdering the souls of men by their corrupt doctrine". The Bible says about Cain:

> ***"And the Lord said to Cain, 'Where is Abel your brother?' And he said, 'I do not know. Am I my brother's keeper?'"***

What an act of arrogance Cain displayed in his response to God. Who talks to God with such arrogance, disrespect, and pride as if they are equal with God. This spirit of rebellion is manifested in different ways in the church today. Some people in the church have out grown correction so much so, that it doesn't matter who is trying to correct them or what they are being corrected about, they simply would not give hid to correction and instruction. They will puff up, they will resist it and they walk away like Cain in arrogance. They do not have teachable spirit because they want to follow the ways of Cain. In other words, they want to do things their own way. What is the point of the comparison? Cain is supposed to be introduced as the type of murderous envy, of the persecuting spirit, or of those who live by the impulse of nature, regardless of God or man. A wickedness defying God and destroying man.

A lesson that we can learn from God's reaction to Cain's offering is that no matter how you would like to do things your own way; God is very selective of what you give to Him at a righteous altar as well as the manner in which it is presented. So JESUS knowing the will of His Heavenly Father taught us in Matthews gospel that; when you are bringing an offering to God and you notice a brother have ought against you; he said, leave your offering at the altar and go and make peace/reconciliation with your brother first. This goes to prove that God is indeed selective in what He accepts and what He rejects. This selective attribute of God is very important because it is what separates the Almighty God from idols (demon-gods) who on the other hand, are so desperate to be worship that they will accept any accursed thing offered to them by their human attendants.

Idols are so desperate for expression in the world of men that they will accept any offering, sacrifice, act of worship regardless of how it is offered, no matter how filthy it is; provided they can gain access to the soul of mankind. God on the other hand is sovereign, holy, and separate from sin and therefore He is particular on what He accepts as offering. This therefore mean that God cannot be manipulated by what we offer to Him at His holy altar. However, we don't hear much any more about this selective attribute of God these days in the church that's why many churches have become a place of no standard. A place where "anything goes"

It is worth noting that whenever there is a deviation in doctrine of the Christian faith, it leads to a deviation from holiness

Let me show you how selective the Almighty God is, from a passage of scripture in the book of Malachi.

Malachi 1;1-8

1 *The burden of the word of the Lord to Israel by Malachi.*
2 *I have loved you, saith the Lord. Yet ye say, Wherein hast thou loved us? Was not Esau Jacob's brother? saith the Lord: yet I loved Jacob,*
3 *And I hated Esau, and laid his mountains and his heritage waste for the dragons of the wilderness.*
4 *Whereas Edom saith, We are impoverished, but we will return and build the desolate places; thus saith the Lord of hosts,* ***They shall build, but I will throw down;*** *and they shall call them, The border of wickedness, and, The people against whom the Lord hath indignation for ever.*
5 *And your eyes shall see, and ye shall say, The Lord will be magnified from the border of Israel*
6 A son honoureth his father, and a servant his master: if then I be a father, where is mine honour? and if I be a master, where is my fear? saith the Lord of hosts unto you,

O priests, that despise my name. And ye say, Wherein have we despised thy name?
7 Ye offer polluted bread upon mine altar; and ye say, Wherein have we polluted thee? In that ye say, The table of the Lord is contemptible.
8 And if ye offer the blind for sacrifice, is it not evil? and if ye offer the lame and sick, is it not evil? offer it now unto thy governor; will he be pleased with thee, or accept thy person? saith the Lord of hosts.

2. THE ERROR OF BALAAM

The "Error" of Balaam, as indicated in (Jude 1;11) must be distinguished from his "way" as stated in ("2 Pet 2:15") and from his "doctrine" as stated in ("Rev 2:14"). The "error" of Balaam was that, reasoning from natural morality and seeing the evil in Israel, he supposed a righteous God must curse them. In other words, Balaam for the sake of gain and selfish interest, corrupt the word of God and refined away its meaning, and let it down so as to suit the passions of his shamelessly immoral attitude. This was literally true of the Nicolaitans as mentioned in the book of Revelation who advanced the error of Balaam into doctrine, taught most impure doctrines, and followed the most lascivious practices. Balaam made the Israelites to err from the way of righteousness by teaching Balak to cast a stumbling-block before them - to eat things sacrificed to idols, and to commit fornication (Revelation 2:14).

Similar to the actions of Balaam, the desire for gain at all cost propel men forward to many act of wickedness and sin. See what the bible teaches about people who are always in haste to accumulate wealth.

> ***"A faithful man shall abound with blessings; but he that maketh haste to be rich shall not be innocent"* (Proverbs 28:20)**

People who are in haste to be rich shall not be innocent because their haste leads to impatience, and their impatience leads to attaining their goal at all cost, regardless of how and what they do to achieve those goals. Notice that Cain did the same by eliminating his brother Abel through jealousy and in order to gain all for himself. So did Balaam and Korah in their actions against Israel and Moses respectively.

THE DOCTRINE OF BALAAM

Revelation 2:14

> ***"But I have a few things against thee, because thou hast there them that hold the doctrine of Balaam, who taught Balac to cast a stumbling block before the children of Israel, to eat things sacrificed unto idols, and to commit fornication".***

Balaam is not a man of God, whose action or words God would confirm.

He was more of a sooth sayer.
Balak statement in Number 22 verse 6.

> ***"for I wot (wot-: to know, to be aware) that he whom thou blessest is blessed, and he whom thou cursest is cursed".***

Is only Balak's opinion of Balaam, this was not fact. If someone speaks to God and God speaks back to them, it doesn't necessarily mean they have a favorable relationship with God

The bible makes us understand that at times, God talks to people with whom He does not have favorable relationship. Consider the following as examples:

- *God spoke to Cain who killed his brother Abel,*
- *God spoke Abimelech, who He warned not to sleep with Abraham's wife Sarah,*
- *God also spoke to Laban warning him not to hurt or even speak good or bad to Jacob,*
- *God will speak with the heathens, ungodly people or even the wicked, especially to warn them about touching or hurting His people.*

But the mere fact that God spoke to them, does not give them any status of grandeur or privilege before God. In Psalm 105:15 God declares that; "Don't touch my anointed, and neither do any harm to my prophets …."

We should not be so taken by people's opinion of others because an opinion is just what it is, - an opinion. It may be right or wrong regardless of whose opinion it is. The fact that someone says he speaks to God and

God speaks back to them does not guarantee credibility of claim. Even when he is able to predict something that comes to pass, does not mean that the person is a man or woman of God.

1 John 4:1 admonishes us to not believe every spirit, but rather, to try the spirit whether they be of God or not for many false prophets are gone out in the world.

Numbers 23:20-21 Balaam speaks saying

20 Behold, I have received commandment to bless: and he hath blessed; and I cannot reverse it.

After his failure to curse Israel, Balaam said to Balak: ***"I cannot curse these people. But you can get them to curse themselves through enticing them to rebel against their God."***

Send your prettiest girls among them and tell them to entice the men of Israel to immorality and idolatry. And it worked because Chapter 25 opens up with the following statement:

> ***"And Israel abode in Shittim, and the people began to commit whoredom with the daughters of Moab".***

The women of Moab, came among the men of Israel, seduced them to both sexual sin and idolatry by bowing down in worship to their gods.

Notice that sexual sin and idolatry were commonly connected in perverse forms of idol worship in the ancient world. Balaam had done his best to curse Israel but was unsuccessful. Yet, he wouldn't let the matter end because of his love of money.

2 Peter 2:15-16 speaks of Balaam and his love of money, using him as an example of later false prophets.

Revelation 2:14 makes the connection between Balaam's unsuccessful attempt to curse Israel and this subsequent idolatry. This goes to say that; the fierce attack of Satan against us can never do as much damage as compared to our own sin and rebellion against the LORD. The sword of no other, and the curse of no other, had the power to damage Israel. Only Israel herself could bring this misfortune, this distress, this destruction upon herself

In the same manner, Satan's violence and sorcery can have no lasting influence on the believer; but if Satan can lead us into sin, only then shall we become victims of God's judgement. How does he get us? He simply waves the thing we desire or lust after in our faces, and when we are drawn away and enticed it leads to our destruction.

The doctrine of Balaam therefore is that doctrine that teaches your enemies how to get you. It teaches them how...

- *To throw the protection of God off you*
- *To be a hindrance to your own progress*
- *To undo yourself, to unravel yourself*
- *To expose yourself to the enemy*
- *To create your own destruction*

However, as long as you remain in God's favor, no one can fight against you and win. As long as your relationship with God is steady, no outside attack can do much threat to your safety. We are therefore our own worst enemy when we become students of the doctrine of Balaam. Every man is tempted when he is drawn aside of his own lusts. There are always trouble makers around who want to get all up in your face because of your zeal for the Lord. Watch those busy bodies. The adversary always seeks to gain access to our secure space through them. But like Nehemiah in Nehemiah chapter 2 verse 20, we need to start telling busy bodies that, "they have no portion, nor right, nor memorial, in Jerusalem."

In other words, what audacity do they have to have an opinion on what I purposed in my heart to do for God?

Let us take a look in Numbers 31:1-18 of what seem to be the last assignment the God gave Moses to accomplish before He lives the scene as leader of Israel. It was as if God was saying to Moses; "it is time to come home, but I have one last job for you to do before your departure". The charge was that God wanted Moses to deal with those Midianites, who cause Israel to sin before he leaves the scene. Although the Midianites were descendants of Abraham by Keturah (The woman Abraham married after the death of his wife Sarah - Gen. 25:2) some like Jethro settled south of Canaan and retained the worship of the one true God. But these who settled east of Canaan had fallen to Idolatry and confederacy with the Moabites. They sent their women among the Israelites to draw them to whoredom and idolatry. For that provocation, God says to Moses, avenge Israel of the Midianites. The Moabites contributed to the crime, however the Midianites were probably more involved in this mischief of causing Israel to sin.

God had taken vengeance on his own people for yielding to the Midianites' temptations, however, although judgment begin at the house of God, it shall not end there, 1 Peter 4:17

There is a day coming when vengeance will be taken on those that have introduced errors and corruptions into the church, together with the devil who worked in them that deceived men and they both will receive a recompense for their actions.

Note that, God sometimes removes his precious Servants from the scene to spare them from ill, and disaster; but they are usually not removed till they have done the work which was appointed unto them. Such is the likes of Moses. He gave orders to the people to prepare for this expedition and avenge the Lord of Midian.

It is worth noting that the interests of God and Israel are united, and the cause of both is one and the same.

If God, in what he does, shows himself jealous for the honor of Israel, then surely Israel, in what they do, ought to show themselves jealous for the glory of God.

In conclusion, Israel warred against the Midianites. They slew the kings of Midian the same that are called elders of Midian (in Numbers Ch. 22:4), and the dukes of Sihon, Jos. 13:21. Also note that they slew Balaam as_he justly died the death of the wicked. Since the Midianites' wiles were Balaam's projects, it was therefore just that he should perish together with them. It is sad to say that Balaam who foretold the fate of others, did not foresee his own. That is what usually happens to those who live by mischief, they do not see what it is that is coming against them.

3. THE GAIN SAYING OF KORAH

The history of Korah as found in the Old Testament points to the fact that he was a Levite of the tribe of Levi, and cousin-german of Moses. He was, therefore, employed in an honorable department of the ecclesiastical service which is; " to wait upon the sons of Aaron in the service of the house of the Lord." He however took matters into his own hands and opposed the exclusive privileges of Moses and Aaron, saying that they "took too much upon them," in order to claimed the privileges of the priesthood for himself and others as indicated by Moses' remarks to Kora; "And seek ye the priesthood also?" says Moses. His ultimate design together with Dathan, Abiram and the others is to masked the present order by putting forward claims to spiritual equality on behalf of every Israelite and so he said in the verse 3 of Numbers 16; ".......*Ye take too much upon you,* ***seeing all the congregation are holy, every one of them, and the LORD is among them: wherefore then lift ye up yourselves above the congregation of the LORD?"***

The conduct of Korah finds its counterpart in Jude's day, through people who despised the ordinances of the Church, and set at naught the order of the Church. This they did to show contempt for Divine order and appointment. Since the Aaronic priesthood was of divine appointment; thus in rejecting it, the conspirators were really rebelling against God. God took the matter into His own hands because it was a rebellion against Him, more than Moses.

Numbers 16:30

But if the LORD make a new thing, and the earth open her mouth, and swallow them up, with all that appertain unto them, and they go down quick into the pit; ***then ye shall understand that these men have provoked the LORD.***

These rebels wished to set up a priesthood and a sacrificial system of their own; and God never has blessed, and never can bless, any scheme of salvation which is not of his own appointment. Their actions showed their discontentment with their existing privileges; envy at the divinely appointed leaders of the Church and ingratitude to God for their privileges. It is worth noting that God opposes those who oppose his ordinances according to Proverbs 24:22

> ***"An evil man seeketh only rebellion, therefore a cruel messenger shall be sent against him"***

Jude described the sin of Korah as 'gainsaying' which is a denial of the authority of Moses as God's chosen spokesman, and intrusion into the priestly office of Aaron. The term which is very fitly rendered "gainsaying" denotes properly an opposition expressing itself in words. It lies in the broader sense of a contemptuous and determined assertion of self against those that are divinely appointed by God.

Gainsaying has its' root from the word *antilogia. 'Anti'* means *against and 'logos'* mean *word*. In effect gainsaying means to speak against. Hence, gainsaying literally means to contradiction what one is saying, such as Korah did against Moses in Numbers 16:3. Korah, by his actions, became a ringleader of the rebellion, by persuading Dathan, Abiram, and their company of 250 men, in Numbers 22) to joined with him, in actions that affected the priesthood, undermined the divinely appointed role of Moses and Aaron as well as rose up seditiously against Moses and Aaron. This error of Korah, Dathan and Abiram was first recorded in the book of Numbers is one among many other errors that has repeatedly been referred to more than any other in both the Old and New Testament. References to this particular event has been referred to either directly or indirectly in Numbers 26:9, Deuteronomy 11:6, Psalms 106:16, and Jude 1:11. This goes to show that their rebellion against the leadership that God had set over His people was so distasteful to God to say the least and the judgement of God that followed their actions attest to that fact. For this error, God brought upon them judgement as have never been brought upon any other human being in the history of humanity. For their rebellion, the earth opened its mouth and swallowed Korah, Dathan and Abiram alive into Hades (Hell). However, notice that God's punishment to the 250 men that followed after them were lesser in severity. They were instead, consumed by fire. This goes to show that God holds his leaders to a higher standard than the people who follow them. The Aaronic priesthood was of divine appointment; and thus in rejecting it, the conspirators were really rebelling against God.

CHAPTER FOUR

BLOOD AND FIRE

From the previous chapter, I tackled the reason why Abel's offering was accepted by God while Cain's offering was rejected. However, in this chapter, I will be dealing with an even more pressing issue than the acceptance and rejection of Abel and Cain's offerings respectively. The Bible account of the story of Cain and Abel as narrated in the fourth chapter of the book of Genesis did not leave us with any clues as to exactly how the two brothers were able to ascertain whether their offerings have been accepted or rejected except for the fact that the Bible mentioned in passing as indicated in the verses 4b-5 below that;

> ***"4 .... the LORD had respect unto Abel and to his offering:***
> ***5 But unto Cain and to his offering he had not respect...."***

Therefore, the even bigger question to answer in this twist of a story is; "How did Abel know that his offering has been accepted by God, and also how was Cain able to know the fact that his offering was rejected?" I do not believe that the two brothers heard a voice declaring from heaven as it was in the case of Jesus' baptism or else the Bible would have stated that clearly. Neither do I believe that there was a pre-existing tradition that was passed on to Cain and Abel because the book of Genesis did not make mention of any burnt sacrifices offered by their father Adam. Therefore, the answer to the question of how Cain and Abel got to know whether their gifts have been accepted or rejected must be supported by at least one or more scriptural references, or else it will not be based on a solid doctrinal grounds. Since there were no other sacrifices made that pre-dates that of Cain and Abel, the answer to this question can be only deduced from similar events in the Bible that post-date Cain and Abel's sacrifice. Through that, one can establish a pattern of what signals God's acceptance or rejection of sacrifice or burnt offering.

Here is the answer to the question as to how Cain and Abel were able to ascertain the outcome of their offerings:

> ***"whenever God accepts an offering, God sends down His fire from heaven upon the offering to consume it".***

In a moment, I will provide you with some proof of this divine principle of God from the pages of the holy scriptures. These proofs will then also serve as the basis for the answer provided above. *For* Abel's burnt offering to be deemed as acceptable, it means that when Abel placed his offering before God, the fire of God must have come down to consume it. This is what signifies God's acceptance. In contrast, upon the offering of Cain, there was no fire sent down from heaven. Also, notice that when Abel gave his offering, blood was shed because he slew a lamb from his flock's firstling. While on the other hand, no blood was shed as a result of Cain's sacrifice. In effect, Abel had the two necessary components or critical ingredients present in his offering. He had blood and the fire of God present for the sacrifice to be consumed, while his brother Cain had none of the two.

Therefore, the fundamental divine principle at play here is that, whenever God accepts blood offerings, God also sends down His fire from heaven to consume that sacrifice. Always! Always! Down comes the fire when God sees the blood. Therefore, based on this fundamental divine principle of Blood and Fire, I would like to give you a few notable examples from the Bible beginning from the offering of Abel which was consummated by fire from heaven as a sign of God's endorsement and acceptance. It's worth noting that the acceptance of Abel's offering was the first of its kind because we never read about Adam making any such offerings unto the Lord and neither were there any accounts in the Bible whereby an offering made by Adam was accepted or rejected by God. Therefore, the only way for Abel to know that his offering had been accepted was through God's response to his offering, and what was that response from God? This response was the sending down of fire from heaven to consume Abel's offering. God showed His respect and approval to Abel's offering and that was through the fire of God that was sent down from heaven upon the offering. There was no other way to ascertain God's acceptance or rejection than God's reaction to the offering of Abel.

Since then, God's order has always been *the blood first, followed by the fire*, and then after that, any other kind of offerings can follow. However, this divine order of the blood first, followed by the Fire, is critical and would later play out evidently in other notable offerings and sacrifices in the Bible on different occasions, dispensations, and by various servants of God. Notice that Abel was just the first, but not the last because, after Abel, God followed the same divine pattern or order of blood first and then Fire second.

Here are a few notable Bible examples that I have put together to prove God's divine principle of blood first, followed by Fire.

1) The Sacrifice of Elijah and the Fire of God.

Now, I hope you do recall that remarkable account in 1 Kings 18, about how Elijah challenged all the Priests of Baal? Elijah, knowing the divine principle of God discussed in this chapter, challenged the prophets of Baal to make up their minds either to serve the true God, Jehovah or to continue in the vile worship of Baal, which Ahab and his wife, Jezebel, had thrust upon the people. Elijah then brought the people to a challenge at Mt. Carmel. Elijah's challenge to the priest of Baal was simple and straight forward. He said to them; - "Let *the God who answers by fire, be acknowledged as the real God*". He as well said to more than six hundred priests of Baal, "You are many, I am one. We will both make a sacrifice. You shall take a bullock and offer it on your altar and to your God, and then call on Baal your God to bring the fire down to consume the sacrifice. After which Elijah promised that he will also take a bullock and put it on the Lord's altar, and call upon the God of Israel." I believe Elijah threw this challenge to the Prophets of Baal because he understood something that Cain did not understand; and that is, it takes the blood on the altar to bring down the fire of God.

He said to the prophets of Baal, "We will both offer sacrifices unto our God's and whosoever's God answers by fire, let Him be the real and true God who ought to be worshipped". As the story goes, the prophets of Baal set up their offering first and started to call upon their gods from day-break till the evening but there was no answer from their gods and neither was there any fire to indicate that their gods had answered their call. The priests of Baal labored, cutting themselves with knives until their blood leaked on the altar they had erected.

Therefore, Elijah mocked them, saying, perhaps Baal is asleep although a true deity will not sleep. He also said to them, maybe your God is on a hunting expedition. Maybe your voices are not loud enough to be heard, so he encouraged them to cry out even louder so their gods could listen to them. Elijah further mocked them by saying; perhaps their gods were asleep and had not woken up from a deep sleep as yet. He, therefore, encouraged them to cry out even louder at the top of their voices.

These poor, confused, and foolish priests of Baal couldn't even see that Elijah was making a mockery of them and their gods by his words of encouragement. To my uttermost surprise, the verse 28 says; the priests of

Baal followed the advice of Elijah whom they were in competition with, and *"**they cried out loud**"* and they started to cry louder until they began to cut themselves out of frustration resulting from a lack of answer from their gods. This is because people who serve idols are always confounded and confused. The Bible says in Psalm 97:7 ***"Confounded be all they that serve graven images, that boast themselves of idols…".***

Baal's priest was obviously confused because when you are in a competition with another party, it is not normal and wise to take counsel from the opponent because it may lead to your demise.

After all Prophets' attempts to get their gods to answer their cry failed miserably, Elijah now began to set up his offering unto the one true God of Israel. Finally, Elijah prepared an altar, building it up with the twelve stones, representing the twelve tribes of Israel, and unhewn stones as God had commanded in the old days. Elijah first killed the bullock. He strangely called for water to pour over the sacrifice before calling down fire from heaven. Therefore, Elijah covered the altar with water to make it even more difficult for the God of Israel to rise to the occasion. But as noted by the disciple Luke, *"**For with God, nothing shall be impossible" (Luke 1:37).***

It is worth noting that Elijah made a ditch underneath his offering and poured water unto the wood. This act made it impossible for an offering to catch fire under natural and ordinary circumstances. Water is always a fierce opponent to fire, and that explains the reason why fire is quenched by the use of water. The Spiritual Interpretation of Elijah's action is that by pouring water on the wood, he made the wood's ability to catch fire impossible. This made the circumstances surrounding the offering naturally impossible. It is interesting to note that his actions were invoking the presence of God. This is because God specializes in the impossibility.

> ***"By soaking the altar with water, Elijah was invoking a very important attribute of God, which is, God's ability to do that which is impossible."***

This attribute of God runs through scripture in both the Old and the New Testaments. On many occasions in the Bible, God waits until the situation becomes humanly helpless and impossible before He brings divine intervention. There are many examples in the Bible and your life that prove that indeed specializing in impossibilities is one of the greatest attributes of the Most-High God. Just to name a few examples:

- When Jesus was informed about the illness of Lazarus, Jesus waited till Lazarus was dead before He approached the home of Mary and Martha. And so after the impossibility had been invoked, then came the miracle of raising Lazarus from the dead.

- On another occasion, Jesus was called upon by a man named Jairus to heal his sick daughter. Jesus was interrupted by the woman with the issue of blood. When Jesus was done interacting with this needy woman, messengers brought word from Jairus' household that Jairus' daughter was dead. Here again, as in the case of Lazarus, it was after an impossible climate had been established that the miracle of raising Jairus' daughter from the dead occurred.
- Even in the case of the woman with the blood issue, it was after she had spent all her living on finding a cure and nothing got better that she received her miracle through the touching of the hem of Jesus' garment.

At times, God brings us to the point of zero and the place of emptiness before He intervenes in our situation and shows forth His glory in our lives.

This, therefore, explains what I have come to term, *"The mystery of the zero factor."* This is because invoking the impossibility also invokes the presence of God. Shadrach, Meshach, and Abednego were placed under circumstances that made it impossible for any mortal being to go through and live. They were placed in a furnace that was heated seven times its standard capacity. And it was only after the impossibility of their survival was evoked that God showed up as the fourth man in the fiery furnace. My question to you is that, are you going through some emotional situation in your life right now? If you are, I encourage you to never give up on your faith in God no matter how helpless and hopeless the situation may seem. The delay in God's intervention, may be because God is waiting for your case to reach the realm of 'impossibility' before he shows up on your behalf.

The conclusion to this story is that after Elijah had set up the wood and sacrifice unto the Lord, he lifted up his hands and prayed unto the Lord. God sent fire from heaven to consume the sacrifice despite the presence of the water around the sacrifice. So here as in the case of Abel, you can see that God always sends down His fire of approval from heaven whenever He sees blood sacrifice offered from a pure heart.

2) Solomon's Offering and the Fire of God

This occurred after God had forbidden King David from building the temple and instead allowed his son Solomon to build Him a temple. God did not let King Solomon's father and predecessor in the person of King David to do it because David had too much blood on his hands. This story is recorded in 2 Chronicles 7. After King Solomon had labored for several years to build the temple of the Lord, the Bible says that during the occasion of the dedication of the temple, when Solomon had made an end to his prayers, the glory of the Lord filled the house of God and the fire of God came down from heaven and consumed the burnt offerings and the sacrifices that were laid upon the altar of God. Here again, like in the case of Abel and Elijah's sacrifice, we see the divine principle of blood first and then followed by the Fire of God at play.

3) Abraham's sacrifice and the fire of God.

The third example in the Bible where the principle of blood followed by fire occurred was in Genesis chapter 15. This was on the occasion of God's covenant made with Abraham. After God had entered into a covenant with Abraham about the miraculous birth of Isaac and what will befall the posterity of Abraham through his descendants, he questioned God on how he was going to inherit what God had promise.

Genesis 15:8 ***"And Abraham said, Lord God, whereby shall I know that I shall inherit it?"***

In response, God instructed Abraham to offer a blood sacrifice using the type and kind of animals that the Lord had prescribed for the sacrifice in the ninth verse of Genesis, chapter 15.

Gen. 15:9 ***"And the Lord said unto Abraham, take me am heifer of three years old, and she goat of three years old, and a ram of three years old, and a turtledove, and a young pigeon.***

10. And he took unto him all these, and divided them in the midst, and laid each piece one against another: but the birds divided he not.

Therefore, going back to Abram's sacrifice in Genesis 15, and verse 17,

17. And it came to pass, that, when the sun went down, and it was dark, behold a smoking furnace, and a burning lamp that passed between those pieces.

18. On the same day, the LORD made a covenant with Abram, saying, unto thy seed have I given this land, from the river of Egypt unto the great river, the river Euphrates.

Like the other instances given above, note that although the material for the sacrifice came from Abram, the fire that consumed the sacrifice came from God. Abram did not set the sacrifice on fire. According to verse 17, it was God who sent forth fire to consume the sacrifice laid on an altar by Abram.

So the divine principle at play in all these occasions is that ***"whenever God accepts an offering, God sends down His fire from heaven upon the offering to consume it.***" Therefore, going back to Cain and Abel's sacrifices, what should they have done for God to accept the offering of both brothers? This is what I believe they should have done. They should have both come together and first and foremost offer together a sacrifice with a lamb from Abel's flock. Then together, they could have proceeded to present the first fruits from the best of Cain's harvest.

In other words, Cain should have joined with his brother Abel in the offering of the lamb. Abel should have likewise joined with Cain in the offering of the first fruits, for that's God's order of things. The blood always comes first before anything else. By so doing, the blood offering covers both of them and the fruit offering as well will cover both of the brothers. The blood sacrifice should always come first and be acceptable to God before any other gifts offered unto God. That's why the Apostle Paul admonished the Church in Rome to first present their bodies as a living sacrifice unto the Lord, which according to the Apostle Paul, will serve as their reasonable service because God's divine order of things will not change.

First Things First.

When the lamb's sacrifice has been made and accepted, then one can come and offer the first fruits unto God. This is because the lamb sacrifice produces blood, and it is the only blood that can atone for humanity's sins and make a man acceptable before God. It's worth noting that both the lamb offering and the gift offering are sacrifices. However, the principle God is teaching us here is that; Some things come before others, and that man cannot change God's order of things nor appease God in any other way besides His ordained way.

Today, we have many people who offer sacrifices in the form of singing and producing gospel albums without first believing in the atoning sacrifice that Jesus Christ provided with His own blood on Calvary's cross. Their gifts are, therefore, nothing more than lip service.

And so today, we see many people who have no spiritual connection with God through the blood of

Jesus, offering lip services in songs unto the Lord. How can you sing of the God you never know or have never had any personal experience with? These people who claim to be singing gospel music and yet have no relationship with the God they are singing about are merely trying to place other sacrifices above and beyond the blood sacrifice of Jesus Christ on Calvary. Still, with God, it is the blood that speaks for the atonement of our sins, and it is the same that makes us acceptable before His holy presence.

The New Testament application is that; "God is not willing to accept any of your first fruits or lip services until one has come to know Him and accept Him through Jesus Christ. That is not until you've been to Calvary and been washed by the blood of the Holy Lamb of God. Apostle Paul says in his letter to the Romans, "*I beseech you, brethren, by the mercies of God, that ye present your bodies a living sacrifice, holy, acceptable unto God*" **(Romans 12:1)**.

But presenting your bodies as a living sacrifice is only useful after you've been to Calvary! Unless the blood is marked upon you, any other offering you give is unacceptable to God.

Therefore, all the talk about:

- *making Jesus your Healer,*
- *making Jesus your Friend,*
- *making Jesus your Comforter,*

doesn't mean a thing until one first accepts the blood sacrifice of Christ for their sins. It's the blood that makes atonement for the soul of man.

CHAPTER FIVE

WHERE IS THE FIRE?

In chapter three, I established the foundation for the divine principle of blood first and fire second. I also showed and expounded that whenever God accepts a blood sacrifice, He places His seal of approval on it by sending down fire from heaven to consume the sacrifice. I then gave examples of significant and notable occasions in the Bible where God sent down His fire of approval to consume sacrifices made unto Him on the altar.

In this chapter, I would like to offer you the third and final example of the divine principle of blood first and fire second established in the previous chapter. This example has to do with our Lord Jesus Christ Himself, and it is the epitome of all the other models already given and any other that may exist in the Bible. Since the offering of His own Blood on Calvary's cross officially marks the end to all blood sacrifices in both the Old and New Testaments, I decided to devout this entire chapter to expound on it.

4) The Offering of Jesus and Fire

The nineteenth chapter of the gospel, according to John, tells us of how Jesus was sacrificed as God's holy and only lamb. As we all know, the death of Jesus Christ on the cross of Calvary was not accidental. He offered Himself as everything needed for the final offering and atonement of the sins of humanity once and for all. Everything needed for that final offering was found in Him. It is worth noting that through the laying down of His own life, Christ Jesus became the altar, the Sacrificial Lamb, as well as the High Priest. He offered Himself without spot and wrinkle unto God.

According to biblical accounts of His crucifixion, death, burial, resurrection, blood flowed from His wounded head, upon which the crown of thorns was placed. Also from His bleeding back, sides, hands, and feet. So, it is evident that blood offering was made on the cross. However, there was no fire from heaven to consume the sacrifice that was made at that point.

After His crucifixion, he rose from the dead back to life on the third day as He had promised and recorded by biblical accounts of eyewitnesses. However, there was no fire sent from heaven as a sign to acknowledge the sacrifice made on Calvary's cross.

Jesus spent forty days on earth with his disciples after He had risen. He ascended into the heavens and was received by a host of angels. It was witnessed by His disciples, and others gathered on Mt. Olives. Yet, there was no fire sent down from heaven to attest to the fact that God had accepted Christ's blood sacrifice.

If the divine principle established in the previous chapter holds true, and if it is still in force during the time of Christ efficacious sacrifice, then the big question is, Christ has offered a Blood sacrifice but where is the fire from heaven that's supposed to follow on as God's seal of approval and acceptance of His gift? For the divine principle established in the previous chapter to be accurate, fire from heaven had to accompany His blood sacrifice to align with the focus of 'Blood first, fire second'. This is because, in the case of Abel's blood offering, it was consumed by fire from heaven. In the case of the Prophet Elijah's blood offering on Mt. Carmel, it was consumed from the altar by fire from heaven. Also, in the case of King Solomon's blood sacrifice offered during the dedication of the temple, it was as well consumed from the altar by fire from heaven. Therefore, where is the fire of God in the case of the sacrifice offered by Jesus Christ the Son of God? I will show you in a moment that indeed God did send His fire of approval down from heaven to consume the Blood sacrifice made by our Lord Jesus Christ, just like God did for every one of the examples cited in this chapter.

The Bible says in the book of Acts chapter two that when the day of Pentecost has fully come, some 120 disciples and followers of Jesus Christ, including Jesus' own mother Mary, were gathered together in one place in the Upper Room and with one accord and then suddenly;

> ***"there came a sound from heaven as of mighty rushing wind and filled all the house where they were sitting;***

> ***And there appeared unto them cloven tongues like fire, and it sat upon each of them. They were filled with the Holy Ghost and began to speak with other tongues, as the Spirit gave them utterance.***

Without a shadow of a doubt, the cloven tongues of fire, according to the account of the event that happened on the day of Pentecost, came directly from heaven.

Therefore, like the other sacrifices where God sent fire from heaven as a sign of approval, God did the same to acknowledge the sacrifice of Jesus. This was done by sending down fire on the day of Pentecost.

There wouldn't have been Pentecost without Calvary. The two together are absolutely necessary. However, Calvary always comes first.

Pentecost is only a part of the story that began from Calvary. Pentecost is not complete by itself unless the Pentecost experience is based on Calvary's experience. In other words, there cannot be Pentecost without Calvary. Don't you ever forget that fact because everything that happened in Pentecost was only God's sign of approval of the actual work of atonement that started in Calvary.

Therefore, based upon this fact, the songwriter wrote the words of the following hymn;

1] King of my life, I crown Thee now
Thine shall the glory be
Lest I forget Thy thorn-crowned brow
Lead me to Calvary

Chorus
Lest I forget Gethsemane
Lest I forget Thine agony
Lest I forget Thy love for me
Lead me to Calvary

2] May I be willing, Lord, to bear
Daily my cross for Thee
Even Thy cup of grief to share
Thou hast borne all for me.

I also want to share with you something else that the Holy Spirit brought to my attention about the Pentecost experience. Notice that there appeared upon them cloven tongues of fire first. Then they received the utterance by the Spirit to speak in divers kinds of languages! Don't forget that part because it is the most essential part of the series of events on the day of Pentecost! The cloven tongues as of fire came upon them first, and then followed the utterance to speak in diverse languages. It is not the other way round. It is not the divers kind of tongues first and the cloven tongues of fire second. Again, it is the cloven tongues of fire first, followed by the utterance for them to speak in divers kinds of tongues. This order makes all the difference between an authentic Pentecost experience and a shady one.

You may be wondering why this order and why it is so important. What came upon the disciples who were gathered in the upper room on the day of Pentecost was not just the ability to speak with new tongues. It was the cloven tongues of fire. In other words, the divers' kinds of tongues that they spoke was only a by-product of the cloven tongues as of fire that settled upon them. Meaning, the Holy Spirit of God's focus was not to just give them some strange language to speak in. The Spirit's direction was to bring upon them the heavenly fire that consumes the sacrifice that was made back in Calvary. The Spirit's focus was to endow them with power through the fire of God, sent down upon them from heaven. It was meant to burn carnality and purify their flesh to prepare them for the work set ahead of them. Also, the suffering that some of them were about to endure for the sake of their faith in Christ Jesus.

But it is so sad that in today's Church many have either forgotten or ignored the essence of Pentecost which is the fire of God. However today, all we hear about in the Church when people speak about the Pentecost experience is the speaking in tongues. Why is it that we don't hear much any more about the fire of Pentecost? Why is anyone hardly talking about the cloven tongues of fire that came down on that faithful day of Pentecost? Why has the entire Pentecost experience melted down and been reduced to just the speaking in new tongues and nothing more, while as a matter of fact, the speaking in tongues is only a by-product of the fire that came down on the day of Pentecost?

Note that the cloven tongues of fire is not the same as the divers' kinds of tongues they spoke in, because the father's promise was not about speaking in tongues. It was about being endowed with fire. So putting Pentecost in its right perspective, Pentecost is supposed to be a 'fire-experience' and not a 'tongues-speaking experience.' I do not doubt that they spoke in tongues on the day of Pentecost. Neither do I have any objection to speaking in tongues today when people receive the gift of the Holy Spirit. I am trying to establish here that Pentecost is a 'fire-experience' that is made physically evident by the speaking in tongues. Whenever this order is circumvented, there is the tendency to make the significant facts about the Pentecost experience minor and the minor facts significant. This, I believe, is an error that has been propagated by some elements in the Church for a long time.

To confirm that Pentecost's essence was the fire that came down, John the Baptist's prophetic utterance from God was about why the Holy Spirit was given to the New Testament Church. Very clear and straightforward, John said, ***"He (referring to Jesus) shall baptize you with the Holy Ghost and fire."***

It didn't say that He shall baptize you with the ***Holy Ghost*** and ***tongues***, did he? It was clear that John's emphasis was on fire and not the physical evidence of the fire, which in this case, is the tongues.

> ***"No matter how much we may desire God and the things of God, it is always our flesh that hinders us and causes us to shy away from the power that the fire of God brings into our lives."***

So, if Pentecost is all about the fire, why have the New Testament Church left out Pentecost's fire and instead have been focusing on the divers' kinds of tongues? This is an interesting question, but the answer to this question is very simple and straightforward. The carnal man does not mind speaking in tongues but has always avoided the fire of God that purges the flesh and the self-will of man. Since carnality still hates going through the fire of God, it has the tendency to settle for the speaking in tongues and does not make any attempt to go beyond that physical experience. Isn't that true? – just be honest with yourself.

This is what the Apostle Paul said about carnality; It's ***"not subject to the law of God, neither indeed can be" (Romans 8:7).*** I am not in any way negating or belittling the speaking of tongues in the Church. Neither am I underestimating the experience of speaking with new tongues when one receives the gift of the Holy Spirit. However, the actual promise of Pentecost is not about speaking in tongues. It is about being baptized with the fire of God. The authentic Pentecost experience lies in the endowment and empowerment of the born-again Believer, and that only comes through the fire of God.

Do I believe that they did speak in tongues on the day of Pentecost? Of course, I do! Do I think that God has repeated that spiritual experience hundreds and thousands of times after the first Pentecost? Yes, I do; however, what I do not believe in, is esteeming the minor things about the Pentecost experience over the significant purpose. God is more concerned about dealing with His people's carnality and having His people purged from all fleshy and carnal desires by the fire of God, rather than having us speak with divers kinds of tongues.

That is why many in the Church speak in tongues but have no power. It explains why many speak with tongues and are full of a bad attitude, worldliness, and profanity. Many are insensitive to the Spirit of God because they have not allowed the fire of God to purge their hearts and minds in Christ Jesus. I have met so many that speak with tongues in the Church, but their lives and attitude are such a shame to behold! When they open their mouths, their words are full of venom, yet their tongues are heard louder than any worshipper during Sunday services. Which of the two would you prefer if there was only one choice? If I had a choice between the two, I would rather have the fire of God burning in my heart than rattling in an unknown language that I do not understand. Give me the fire first and then add the tongues later. However, if I have a single choice between the two, I will rather pursue God's fire instead of speaking with new tongues.

When the physical members of your body and the self-will are purged through the fire of God at Pentecost, you will then develop a pure heart towards God. The gift and fruit of the Spirit then begin to flow freely through you. But that only happens when you have your spiritual priorities set right, causing things to start to fall into the right perspective and proper spiritual order.

CHAPTER SIX

CLEANSING BY FIRE

Since I am still on the subject of the fire of God, let me take some time to delve a little deeper into the role of the fire in the life of the true Christian.

The Significance of Fire

Calvary was followed by the fire coming down at Pentecost. Notice that in Abel's case, in Solomon's case, in Elijah's case, as well as in Calvary's case, the same order prevailed. Therefore, what does the presence of the fire mean? What spiritual role does it play in the life of the Believer?

- The fire simply attests to the validity of the sacrifice. It is always an indication that God has accepted the sacrifice. Despite the role of the fire, the blood always comes first. Pentecost would not have meant a thing, except that there was first a Calvary. What is the central doctrine of Christianity? It's not Pentecost, it is Calvary. Let us examine what the Apostle Paul wrote about that.

The Apostle Paul said, ***"God forbid that I should glory, save in the cross of our Lord Jesus Christ" (Galatians 6:14).***

This means we are not to glory in anything else except in the cross of Calvary. Yet, some people are glorying in their gifts of miracle, healing, prophesy, and more.

Remember that the order is as follows; Calvary's cross leads to Pentecost and not the other way around.

> ***The centrality of the cross always keeps the Church in balance. Whenever it is missing in the Church, things begin to fall apart spiritually.***

Isaiah Cleansed by Fire

First, let's consider the Prophet Isaiah's experience as an example of cleansing by fire. We read in the sixth chapter of the book of Isaiah 6:1-6

1. *In the year that King Uzziah died, I saw also the Lord sitting upon a throne, high and lifted up, and his train filled the temple.*
2. *Above it stood the seraphim: each one had six wings; with twain he covered his face, and with twain he covered his feet, and with twain he did fly.*

3. *And one cried unto another, and said, Holy, holy, holy, is the Lord of hosts: the whole earth is full of His glory.*
4. *And the posts of the door moved at the voice of him that cried, and the house was filled with smoke.*
5. *Then said I, Woe is me! for I am undone; because I am a man of unclean lips, and I dwell in the midst of a people of unclean lips: for mine eyes have seen the King, the Lord of hosts.*
6. *Then flew one of the seraphim unto me, having a live coal in his hand, which he had taken with the tongs from off the altar:*
7. *And he laid it upon my mouth, and said, Lo, this hath touched thy lips; and thine iniquity is taken away, and thy sin purged.*

The above text's significance is in the opening verse: ***"In the year King Uzziah died."***

To fully understand this text, one must first find out why and how King Uzziah died. It is worth noting that King Uzziah died before his time of leprosy, which is a sickness that symbolized a curse in those days. Why did he die? He died because as King, he'd actually gone into the temple, taking an incense censer to swing before the Lord, which was a duty reserved solely for the Priest and Levites to do. King Uzziah, therefore, died because he desecrated the temple. After his death, the Prophet Isaiah also realizes that he is standing before the same God in the same temple where King Uzziah had committed his errors. While there, the Prophet Isaiah realized that he too was a sinner and a man of unclean lips and one who dwells among a people of unclean lips. So he declared concerning himself:

"*Woe is me! I am unclean, undone*!"

In the olden days, that was the cry of a leper. In response to the cry of Isaiah for mercy, God sent a Seraphim (Angel), with a live coal in his hand, which he had taken with tongs, off the altar. The Seraphim then placed the coal of fire on Isaiah's lips, and said, *"Lo, this has touched thy lips and thou art clean."*

This is the same principle that I have been discussing in the previous chapter. In this particular instance, God is sanctifying Isaiah's lips by fire because He is the God who answers by fire, which leads to the purification of man's heart. This purification by fire is necessary because God wanted to use Isaiah, not in great deeds of power and mighty miracles like He had done with Elijah, or some other prophets, but by speech. Meaning that Isaiah was going to be a mouthpiece of God. Therefore, after the purification of his lips by fire, Isaiah became perhaps the greatest Prophet of the Old Testament and the one who revealed the most truth about the Messiah.

He revealed the glories of the coming Messiah. He was also the one who told of the Messiah's sacrifice on the cross. Hence for God to speak through Isaiah's lips, they had to be clean lips. That is why God had the fire touch Isaiah's lips, so his heart and lips could be cleansed for the master's use. Isaiah's lips became clean after God touched his lips with the live coal - the tongue of flame that came upon him. If you want to be used by God, you first have to go through the process of purification by fire. God would not use any vessel that is not purified. God will not use you until He can trust what goes into you, thus into your heart, and what comes out of you through your lip. This is because many are those whose utterances have created more division, sentiments, and hatred among members of the body of Christ. Many are those who cause division among God's people rather than bringing unity. Hence God promises in His word that He will give the flock, Shepherds, after His own heart.

The Carnal Mind and Self

The Lord Jesus deals with the carnal mind by removing it because it kicks against God, and it is that part of us that hates God. If you're willing, you can have a pure heart that has no hatred for God. On the contrary, one's self is so weak, so small, and so low. It is one thing for God to cleanse our hearts so that we desire to serve Him. At that point, we're just like Adam was in the Garden of Eden before the Fall, but Adam fell over the tasting of the fruit. Why? Because he was weak through the flesh, and we are the same. Note that Adam did not fall to sin because he had a carnal mind – in fact, he had a pure heart. Instead, he declined because of the weakness of his humanity. He fell because he had a will independent of God. God gave him a great measure of free will, and in that free will always lie the possibility of sin. While the free will God gave to man is one of our greatest gifts from Him, it is also one of the most dangerous gifts humanity received from God. Our free will is precious but also precarious. That may sound contradictory, but I will explain it in a moment.

As much as our will is precious, it can also be a dangerous gift, so we must handle it with much care and caution.

Our free will is precious because when we subject that will to the will of God, we can please God a hundred percent. Also, our free will can be dangerous because that enables us to choose against the God who gave us that will in the first place.

That's how the angels sinned. They had free will. The origin of sin is not in the devil, brothers, and sisters; sin's origin is in humanity's free will.

Now let's consider what a clean heart is. It is a pure heart that only wants to serve its Beloved. As humans, our problem is that we have this beautiful treasure embedded in our flesh. *"this treasure in earthen vessels"* (2 Corinthians 4:7). If you look back to the Garden of Eden, you'll see there were two kinds of sin:

- *the sin of the devil and*
- *the sin of Adam.*

The root of humanity's sin is not hatred towards God but rather love towards the self.

Why did the devil entice Adam and Eve to sin? It's because the devil hated God. On the other hand, why did Adam and Eve sin? Is it because they hated God? Of course not! They loved Him, and they enjoyed the fellowship with God in the cool of the day in the garden of God. They sinned because they turned their attention from God and loved themselves a little above God. That was the sin of self, not the sin of hatred. I hope you got the difference now.

The other was the sin of carnality, which hates God because it is not subject to His law, "neither indeed can be," according to the great Apostle Paul. The devil malignantly led Adam and Eve into sin because he hated them, hated God, hated righteousness, and loved iniquity. But Adam and Eve didn't sin because they loved evil but that they loved themselves too much. Then carnality came upon the human race through their sin.

The love for self is being propagated more than ever in the church world and outside the Church. That is why books, presentations, movies, seminars, etc. on self-actualization have flooded the book market now more than any other time in humanity's history. In some circles in today's society, including the political and entertainment industry, some people call themselves 'image consultants' and whose job it is to project their client's public image. However, it's my desire that instead of projecting my own image, Christ would rather be seen in me. What sort of impression are you projecting as a child of God? Is it the image of the Christ in you the hope of glory, or is it the image of self?

God's remedy for their sin is the Blood of Jesus, and His treatment for carnality is still the same glorious tongue of fire, given initially at Pentecost, and which cleanses us from the carnal mind.

> "***Knowing this, that your old man is crucified with Christ, that the body of sin might be destroyed, that henceforth you might not serve sin" (Romans*** 6:6).

God will chasten you to keep you down, lest you should be trapped again into sin because of the weakness of your human nature. You have the treasure in earthen vessels. He chastens us ***"that we might be partakers of His holiness." (Hebrews, 12:10)***.

In Moses' case, he was to do great signs and wonders. That's why God made him put his hand in his bosom over his heart. Have you noticed that when God's call on the life of Isaiah had to do with the use of his lip, God cleansed his lip? On the other hand, when Moses' call had to do with his hands, God had to cleanse his hands? *Two* signs were given Moses: the first was the throwing down the rod of power, which became God's rod when it was out of Moses' hand. The second sign was that Moses had to put his hand in his bosom over his heart, and when he brought his hand out again, it was leprous. What God is showing here is that the uncleanliness comes from -out of the heart. "Out of the heart," Jesus said, ***"proceed evil thoughts, murders, adulteries, fornications, thefts, false witness, blasphemies"*** **(Matthew 16:19).**

God knows the heart. God knew the heart when He sent the Holy Ghost upon Cornelius. In testifying of what God did at the house of Cornelius, Peter declared, ***"God, which knoweth the heart, bare them, witness, giving them the Holy Ghost even as He did unto us; and put no difference between them and us, purifying their hearts by faith"*** **(Acts 15:7).**

But that was only the Pentecost of the Gentiles. In that Pentecost, God did everything in one short. They were saved, were filled with the Holy Ghost, speaking in tongues, glorified God, and their hearts were made pure through the purging of the Spirit, all at once. That's what some call a blood-red, snow-white, sky-blue salvation. Now, do you see what God did with Isaiah? In Moses' case, God wanted to use Moses' hand on the rod, a rod of power. Therefore, He had to cleanse Moses at the source, so that it was a pure hand from a pure heart, holding out the rod. Fire is destructive; fire is judgment. Fire burns things up and gets rid of the chaff in them. Fire is also a purifying agent. Fire is used to purify metallic substances and to get rid of the impurities in these substances. Even so, what purifies the child of God is the fire of God in their life. It's not supposed to be there for decorative purposes. The Holy Ghost fire was given on the day of Pentecost for no other reason than to purify the desires of the flesh. However, it is sad to know that many believers have turned it into the mere speaking with other tongues.

Preparation for Service

I want to remind you, too, of how the Lord deals with his servants to prepare them for service. Let's look at a few verses in Exodus 3, where the Lord commissioned Moses. The life of Moses can be summarized in three key segments of 40 years each. Moses had lived for forty years in Egypt as the adopted son of Pharaoh's daughter. Then God transferred him, and he lived forty years in the desert with his to be father-in-law Jethro. When he was eighty years old, God considered he was then about ready to do something for Him. How old are you? Do you know, some people have the idea that when you're older, it's time to retire from everything you were once engaged in? They, therefore, retire from secular jobs and from being active in the service of the Lord. Many will spend their so-called retirement age sitting idle in senior daycare centers, playing the indoor game of draft instead of engaging in the work of the Lord. I know of one Church brother who was hardly in Church upon retirement from secular work compared to his attendance before he retired from secular employment. Have you ever met a retired Christian? I mean a real Christian. I never have. There are Some Christians who say, "I'm retired now, so I leave it all to the young people." What are you doing with your life after that? Watching television and the day time shows on TV channels or what?

God decided to begin to use Moses in a leadership role after the age of eighty years. You are not even anywhere near eighty, and you are talking about retirement. You never ever retire! Not in serving the Lord and not in living your life to the fullest. The so-called 'retirement age' is simply a different phase of your life. It is not a phase to stop being active and stop doing all you used to do and just waste away the remainder of your life. "He that has Christ has life," so how can you retire from Christ, who is living and still be alive?

- How can you retire from loving Jesus?
- How can you retire from speaking about Him?
- How can you retire from bringing people to Jesus and bringing them up in their most holy faith?
- How can you retire from being an excellent example unto others who are looking up to you and the experience you have gleaned in life.?

It's like a mother retiring and saying to her children; "Well, children, now that you're married, I relinquish my role as a mother so I don't want to see you all anymore. Every daughter knows that that's when she would need her mother's support the most! Have you retired from serving the Lord because you have a new title known as a retiree? Have you backed down on the things you use to be engaged in Church because someone deceived you that you don't have to be actively involved at a certain age and phase in your life? This is my take on retirement. If Moses' purpose and calling began at the age of eighty, then what do you think you are doing to yourself by beginning to slow down at age 65 years or 70 years although you have the strength to go on. Be on your guard not to fall into the same situation that Isaac found himself in when he presumed that his life was coming to an end soon and therefore based on that presumption, requested his elder son Esau to prepare him his favorite meal so he will eat and bless him.

Genesis 27:1-4

> [1] *And it came to pass, that when Isaac was old, and his eyes were dim, so that he could not see, he called Esau his eldest son, and said unto him, My son: and he said unto him, Behold, here am I.*
> [2] *And he said, Behold now, I am old, I know not the day of my death:*
> [3] *Now therefore take, I pray thee, thy weapons, thy quiver and thy bow, and go out to the field, and take me some venison;*
> [4] *And make me savoury meat, such as I love, and bring it to me, that I may eat; that my soul may bless thee before I die.*

In order words, Isaac was preparing to retire from this life unto death only to found out later that God would permit him to live at least two plus decades after that declaration. Notice that he made that request in Genesis 27:3-4 but then happened to live for over twenty more years thereafter. You cannot live your life preparing to die, until death comes knocking at your door. You have to live with the goal of preparing to live until your appointed time is at hand. Notice that it was upon that request that Jacob deceived Esau and took away his blessings.

After that occasion, Jacob had to escape to live with his uncle Laban.

According to the account of the story, Jacob lived with his uncle for at least twenty plus years until he returned home to meet his father Isaac and eventual to bury him upon the death of Isaac. So it took at least twenty years from Isaac's declaration of nearing his death till he actually passed away. We know that from the span of time that Jacob spent with his uncle while on the run away from his brother Esau. If you quite remember the story, Jacob was tricked to served his uncle seven years in order to be married to Leah and another seven years to be married to Rachel whom he really loved. This gives us a total of fourteen years, not counting the length of time he spent with his uncle before and after the fourteen years. Yet the bible tells us in Genesis 35:27 that Jacob finally returned home to meet his father Isaac still alive.

Genesis 35:27-29

> 27 *And Jacob came unto Isaac his father unto Mamre, unto the city of Arbah, which is Hebron, where Abraham and Isaac sojourned.*
> 28 *And the days of Isaac were an hundred and fourscore years.*
> 29 *And Isaac gave up the ghost, and died, and was gathered unto his people, being old and full of days: and his sons Esau and Jacob buried him.*

It was after Jacob's return that Isaac passed away and was buried by both brothers. So Isaac spent the last years of his life preparing to die, only to find out that God would keep him alive for another twenty years. According to the verse four, Isaac was preparing to 'eat and die' and instead, he ate and live for over twenty more years. That is why it is a waste of time to live preparing to die.

As a pastor, I often get calls to attend to urgent spiritual matters within both members of our congregation and members of the community. At one such occasion, I was called to minister to a terminally ill lady whom Doctors have diagnosed with a stage four cancer and given limited numbers of days left to live. Knowing the spiritual urgency of the situation, I prayerfully when to meet her and her husband in the home, to share the gospel of salvation in Jesus Christ with both of them. To my uttermost surprise, the husband was far more receptive to the message than the lady who was ill and about to die in a matter of months if not weeks or days to come. Beside the fact that she showed no interest in the gospel that I was there to present to them, what surprise me most was the fact that she made several attempts to derailed the conversation and to change the subject of the conversation to what she thought was more important.

So every once a while she will interrupt me and try to tell me about how she has been planning for her own funeral and how she visited the funeral home to choose the color of her casket and to plan the details of her funeral service with the funeral home Director. For the entire time that I was with the couple, this lady did not cease to boost about her efforts to arrange for herself a befitting funeral and burial. It is sad to know that many people are into befitting burial while on the contrary, the word of God admonishes us to live our lives in such a way that we can rather look forward to a befitting resurrection. I would rather that birds eat my body and experience a befitting resurrection upon the sounding of the trumpet of God in the rapture when the dead in Christ shall arise. What is this new fascination with people shopping for burial plots with a nice view and close to the highway etc. As if to say that they will still be physically alive when they die. It is nothing but deception from the enemy of our soul to have us focus on burial instead of the blessed resurrection the Christ has purchase for us on the cross through His atonement.

CHAPTER SEVEN

'NOD'–A STATE OF ISOLATION FROM GOD

In this chapter, I would discuss some life lessons that can be learnt from Cain's errors and from the change of heart that consequently led to his redemption. I would like to begin this chapter by posing the question, "What becomes of a man or woman who walks away from the presence of GOD"?

In the fourth chapter of the book of Genesis (4:8), we are simply told that ***"And Cain spoke to Abel."***

However, it is unclear what he might have said to his brother or what the two spoke about. What they talked about is not reported in the account of the story in Genesis. And notice, the next action after that was that Cain kills his brother Abel. As a lifetime student of the Bible, I understand that nothing in scripture is irrelevant, and nothing is accidental. Also, nothing in scripture tells us anything that we could have known by ourselves. We know Cain spoke to Abel, but we do not see what he said. According to Rabbi Lapin's book *"Business Secrets from the Bible,"* the

Bible doesn't tell us what the two brothers discussed because ancient Jewish wisdom fills in the story for us.

If we are willing to read between the lines, we can figure out what the missing link is in the story of Cain and Abel by judging from the following:

1) *Cain's attitude*
2) *God's warning to Cain.*
3) *Cain's action after the notice.*
4) *By the kind of punishment God imposed upon Cain after he killed his brother.*

In an attempt to read in between the lines, let's begin from what we know and then work our way further up. It's always easier to start from what you know and work your way towards the unknown or the uncertain. So, this is what we know;

- We know that Adam and Eve were getting old, and it was evident that they were going to die at some point in time;
- We know that God had already made it known to them of the imminent death that hangs over their head and from which they cannot escape.

So, Cain being the elder of the two brothers, got hold of Abel, his younger brother, and here's a paraphrase of what I believe he may have said to him in today's' language. *"Hey Bro, as you know, our Dad's going to be on his way soon. Mother's going to be on her way soon as well. That means we will have to inherit the earth. And so I just want to establish with you that since I'm the oldest son, I will be getting everything. You may live wherever you would like to, but you have to pay rent to me as I will assume the role of the rightful owner of everything Mom and Pop leave behind."*

As one will assume, Abel, says in return, "Cain, no way, I don't think you get it. It's not going to be like you are thinking. As a matter of fact, we're going to be splitting it in two all that Mom and Dad leave behind." Cain says, "No, I don't go for your division."
(Taken from Rabbi Lapin's book entitled: "Business Secrets from the Bible")

How does Cain, whose name literally means *acquisition* (possession) and whose only purpose in life is taking from others, react to this refusal? Of course, he eliminates his brother by killing him - this is just his natural choice and the natural tendency of people who want the whole world for themselves. Such people always think eliminating others is their best path to success. Because Cain's name means ***'acquisition,'*** he thinks other people are the obstacle to his ability to acquire wealth. So his only natural choice would be to eliminate his younger brother Abel, so there will be no competitor or competition.

Cain's thought process and deception were that he thinks that the fewer other people in the world, the better off he will be. He believes that if he can get rid of everybody else, he will have everything to himself, but this is a strong delusion that many people fall prey to. Have you ever imagined how difficult life will be for you if you were to live on this earth all by yourself and have no one else to deal with?

Some selfish people think that life will be much better if they don't have a competitor. Everything will automatically fall into their hands without any effort. That's just nothing but a deception and short-sightedness.

Abel wants half, which is his, and obviously, Cain's response was that 'this Abel guy has got to go.'

I believe Cain had other choices in the way he should have handled the situation with his brother. Why would Cain, among all other possible options that he could have taken against his brother, instead want to kill him? Cain could have driven Abel away from the garden of Eden. He could have sold him like Joseph was sold out by his own brothers. He could have kept him on Eden's premises but enslave him and let Abel be his servant. But refused to pursue any of these options and instead ended up killing his brother. This is because Abel's name means "breath," and the only way to eliminate or get rid of breath is to take its life. That's interesting, huh? This looks like a play on words, but it actually brings meaning to the reason why Cain would rather kill his brother than pursue any other course of action against him. There are only three other scriptural references to Cain in the Bible besides the original story's narratives in Genesis's book. However, it is worth noting that every one of the other three scriptures describes Cain in a very hostile and unfavorable manner due to his actions.

When men deviate from God's holy ordinances, there are basically three ways by which evil men orchestrate their evil intentions. The method of Cain, the error of Balaam, or the gainsaying of Kora. None is better than the other because they all lead to the same end result and are all condemned by the Bible in Jude 1:11

> ***"Woe unto them! For they have gone in the way of Cain, and ran greedily after the error of Balaam for reward, and perished in the gainsaying of Core."***

No doubt, Cain's actions against his brother were further described as wicked in I John 3:12, where the Bible says, ***"Not as Cain, who was of that wicked one and slew his brother. And wherefore slew he him? Because his own works were evil and his brother's righteous."***

Notice that, when people are envious of you and want to undermine you, they usually come against you by targeting the qualities that define your life. The things that determine what life means to you and that makes you who you really are. That is the thing they would usually come after and up against. Thus, Cain ends his brother Abel's life and purpose of living by taking his breath away (killing him).

God then punishes Cain in a way that makes him appreciate and understand the error of his ways. This is by isolating Cain and driving him away to the desolate land of Nod.

In my research, I found out that **the name Nod** means to wander, to be tossed to-and-fro, wagging aimlessly, waver, and to totter.

Answering the question, I posed at the beginning of this chapter, "*What becomes of a man or woman who walks away from the presence of the Lord";* The answer is clear and straightforward. Whenever one walks away from the presence of God, that's what one walks into. They move into wandering aimlessly, being tossed to-and-fro by the pain of life without God, by wavering and being unstable as the waves of the sea and more. So, Cain slew his brother to isolate him. As his punishment for his wickedness, God sends him into isolation in a desolate land called Nod. I found out that Nod could possibly be some desolate and remote land created by God just to keep Cain away from Eden. This is because, unlike many Bible locations, Nod's exact location is unknown until this day. It could be a hell on earth that God created to contain and accommodate Cain in his rebellious state. As a result, this is how Cain, in his own words, described his life in Nod; he said, ***"this punishment is unbearable for me.*"**

To conclude this chapter, that is what becomes of a man, woman, boy, girl, brother, or sister who turns their back on God after coming to the knowledge of the truth. You are driven into isolation and from the grace of God, and your life begins to become unbearable, unstable, and without purpose or meaning. That's what happened to Cain when he was driven out of Eden into the land of Nod. Taking residency in the land of Nod is like living a hell on earth. Nod's location was never meant to be a comfortable place for even stubborn and wicked-minded people like Cain.

Do not allow your past mistakes to impede your progress in the future. Take stock of your life and make amendments.

Hence after a while in Nod, Cain decided to amend his ways as a means of making a come-back to typical societal values and relationships with his other fellow men through repentance. This is where his redemption began, and this is also where the story gets even more intriguing. The next chapter deals with how Cain made a come-back from isolation in Nod and the lessons learnt from his past life in Nod and after that.

CHAPTER EIGHT

REDEMPTION STORY

After spending some time in Nod's lonely and desolate land, Cain gradually realized the wickedness of his ways and his past errors. Although he questioned God earlier about whether he is his brother's keeper, Cain began to understand that indeed he is his brother's keeper and that no man is an Island, as the saying goes.

Cain final came to terms after years of isolation in Nod that being around people does not take away from your life or rob you of anything you are supposed to have or be. Rather they enrich your life. With this understanding, Cain began his new journey towards redemption.

We all make mistakes at times, don't we? However, the worse thing than the error itself is to refuse to acknowledge the error and make amendments and to begin to turn around one's ways for the better. The story of Cain gets even more interesting because, in the process of time, the Bible tells us that Cain had a child. He chooses to name the baby ***Enoch,*** or (Hanach) in Hebrew, which means ***'now educated'*** or simply '*dedicated.* His child's birth shows us that Cain had learned his lesson well and is now educated about his past mistakes. By this, there was a clear indication that indeed he had come to acknowledge the fact that we are one another's keeper. Before, Cain thought that having other people around him was contrary to his own interests. Later, he understood that the more the people around him, the more comfortable and better life may be. Just imagine for a moment that you were the only person living on earth. Have you ever imagined how frustrating, lonely, and difficult that may be for you? When you understand in life that you are one another's keeper, you don't compete against your brother or sister; instead, you complement one another.

There is so much *competition* within the Body of Christ because people have not yet come to some basic understanding. That is the fact that we are supposed to guard one another's back. One cannot see nor reach their back because God expects us to look out for each other's good. That is why God, in His wisdom, did not place an eye on the back of our head. God expects your brother or sister to watch your back; hence there is no need to place an eye behind your head. Instead, what we see most of the time is people using one another's weakness as a weapon against them, and that is simply wickedness. The Bible clearly tells us that God hates when one takes advantage of others due to others' weakness, feebleness, or poverty. That's why the word of God cautions us to be kind to the widow, the fatherless, and the poor.

The Spirit of envy and unhealthy competition within the Body of Christ has led to the under-utilization of the gifts, talents, and callings of individuals in the Church.

The Bible says, to 'some' are given the ability to teach. In contrast, others are given the ability to operate in Apostolic ministry or in the ministry of an Evangelist. Today more than ever, the operation of the five-fold ministry of the Church is underutilized because some within the body of Christ are envious of others' gifts and abilities. They will rather ask for the other person's teaching or sermon notes to take away and try to recite it behind the pulpit to their congregation rather than invite the one through whom God has given insight or revelation into a specific subject. On several occasions, I have been asked for my sermon notes instead of being invited in person to deliver the same message. In practice, I am always ready to share my sermon or teaching notes whenever I am asked for it.

Most people fail to understand that a well-written sermon notes is not all that it takes to impart lives from behind the pulpit. For it is the anointing that destroys the yoke.

However, I cannot share what I would like to because it is God's anointing upon my life and ministry, which drives those sermons or Bible teaching notes to yield the result. I applaud Servants of God like Bishop Robert

Henson in Flint, Michigan, Bishop Arthur Thomas in Mt. Vernon, New York, Bishop Dolbert Clarke of the Cayman Islands, and few other Servants of God. They are the type who would humbly say to you; "Brother, I believe God specifically gave you that word to share with the body of Christ, therefore although I could handle it in my own way, I would rather that you come over to share it with my congregation just the way God has given it to you." This is not because these humble servants of God do not have the capability or knowledge to teach or preach on the same bible topics. Instead, it takes the Spirit of humility to acknowledge and accept the diverse gifting and calling in others other than themselves. I firmly believe that the Kingdom of God will be served better if we allow one another's gifts and unique calling to be utilized without prejudice and bigotry.

I am not saying this because I lack the platform or the opportunity to preach or minister in any way or form. Neither am I making references because I am looking to be invited somewhere. On the contrary, I can say this because I usually receive more invitations to speak than I can handle. Due to my current ministerial schedule, my workload as an author, engagement with my secular job outside the pastoral framework, and the several speaking engagements that I received at home in the United States and abroad.

The point I am trying to make here is that the Body of Christ suffers when there are envy and jealousy among the Lord's vineyard's co-laborers. Instead, we ought to be joining forces and resources together and working in harmony with one another to complement each other's gifting and ministry.

Posterity will not forgive us if we fail to advance the Kingdom of God beyond our personal ambitions, no matter what they are. We need to carefully pass on the spiritual legacy handed down to us by those who held it dearly and passed it on to us. With our God-given gifts, talents, current advancement in technology and communication methods, I firmly believe that we can do more, reach more, and accomplish more to better advance the Kingdom of God. We have the window of opportunity through the application of various technologies to win more souls and establish members of the body of Christ rather than pursuing unhealthy competitions against one another in the bid to become well-known or in pursuit of fame and wealth.

Lessons from Hobab.

Allow me to use as an example, a character in the Bible that is least known by many Christians and church-goers alike. The name of this bible character is Hobab, Moses' father-in-law. He is mentioned in Number 10:29 and known as Jethro in other references in the Old Testament.

Numbers 10:29-33 (KJV)

> *29], And Moses said unto* ***Hobab****, the son of Raguel the Midianite, Moses' father in law, we are journeying unto the place of which the Lord said, I will give it to you:* ***come thou with us****, and we will do thee right: for the Lord hath spoken good concerning Israel. [30]* ***And he said unto him, I will not go; but I will depart to my own land, and to my kindred.*** *[31] And he said,*

> *leave us not, I pray thee; (that's a voice of desperation/ frustration) forasmuch as thou knowest how we are to encamp in the Wilderness,* ***and thou mayest be to us instead of eyes****. [32] And it shall be, if thou go with us, yea, it shall be, that what goodness the Lord shall do unto us, the same will we do unto thee* (that is a rain check).
>
> ***[33] And they departed from the mount of the Lord three days' journey: and the ark of the covenant of the Lord went before them in the three days' journey, to search out a resting place for them.***

Notice that although the presence of God was with Moses in the form of the ark, yet Moses and the nation he was chosen to lead out of Egypt, seemed to be lost in the desert. The lesson we can learn from this is that no matter how close one may be to God, it does not mean that you won't have roadblocks at times in your life or that people won't turn their backs on you and reject your leadership at times;

Hobab - His Descent:

Hobab, we know from scripture, was a dark skin man. We are not sure whether he was Jethro's son (Moses' father-in-law) or Jethro himself.

But either way, that does not change his descent because Jethro, we know, was a Medianitish Priest. The *progenitor of the Midianites by name Media* was the son of Abraham through a woman named Keturah because, after Sarah's death, Abraham had six other sons with Keturah, who was a dark-skinned woman.

When Moses, the man with the vision, left Egypt together with Israel and did not know their way through the desert, Moses invited Hobab to lead them through the desert and show them the way because Hobab knew the in-roads through the scourging and dangerous Wilderness.

Disappointing to say, Hobab refused to go with them and that I believe was a missed opportunity not just for Hobab but also for his posterity. This is because you don't necessarily have to be the one with the vision to benefit from it. You can share in a leader's vision and reap the same blessings as the leader.

Let me show you how vital this invitation was and the magnitude of the opportunity missed by Hobab. In verse 31 of Numbers, chapter 10, - we are told that Moses pleaded with Hobab to be the 'eyes' of the young nation that God was about to raise from slavery into greatness.

> ***[31] And he said, Leave us not, I pray thee; (that's a voice of desperation/frustration) forasmuch as thou knowest how we are to encamp in the Wilderness, and thou mayest be to us instead of eyes.***

It is worth noting that Christ's universal body (commonly referred to as the Ecclesia) will always need 'an eye' regardless of the time and dispensation in which the Church finds herself. Whenever you see the Church wandering aimlessly and cannot see her way correctly, you should know that something has gone wrong with those positioned by God to be the eyes of the Church.

Before I go any further with the point that I am trying to establish, let me give you a few more examples of occasions in the Bible where the Church had to wander about and couldn't find its way simply because it was blind.

1. Pastor Moses and the children of Israel, while they were lost in the Wilderness, are examples of the Church in the state of blindness.
2. Pastor Sampson, with his eyes plucked out in the heathen courts, was also a type and shadow of the Church in the state of blindness.
3. Furthermore, Jesus Christ with a crown of thorns on his head and His own blood dripping down into his eyes while staggering on a wooden cross towards Calvary, was also an example of the Church in a state of blindness.

One can only expect to share in the leader's blessing when they share in their vision. So what you need to do is to align yourself with the person with the idea.

Besides asking Hobab to be their eye through the Wilderness; Moses also offered Hobab a 'rain check' of promise when Moses said to Hobab, and I believe to his posterity as well; "***We will likewise bless you with whatever blessings the Lord blesses us with; so please, come with us and be to us an eye through the wilderness.***"

In other words, Moses was inviting Hobab to lead them through the unchartered Wilderness since he knew the in-roads of the desert better. In a way, he was also asking him and his descendants after him to be partakers of God's blessings that will be bestowed upon the nation Israel in the future. Hobab's assistance was crucial because he knew the short-cuts and the dangerous places where Israel ought not to tread. As one would expect, there are possibly venomous snakes, scorpions, and other creatures in the hot sandy desert beside the dangerous sand dunes that, at times, act like land-mines.

This leads me to the main point I want to make by mentioning Hobab as an example. Hobab found himself amid something great, and the sad thing is that he did not even recognize the essence of the moment he was in. This is what causes many people to miss their date with destiny.

Let me pause and emphasize that we have to be watchful not to miss the special moments that will elevate us into our destiny. "You can be in the midst of what could perhaps lead to the most incredible window of opportunity or blessings, or even maybe the best thing that will ever happen in your lifetime, and if you are not watchful, you may miss the chance. That's what happened to Hobab because that moment with Moses and the nation of Israel was not just about Hobab. Seizing the opportunity through Moses' invitation to lead them would have also brought about God's covering, blessings, and prosperity to his descendants after him. However, it is sad to say that he missed such a great opportunity because he could not see the forest for the trees.

He missed what would have been his moment with Destiny. Therefore, one would notice that Hobab's name did not surface in the Old Testament from that moment. Also, there were no further references about him in the pages of scripture. He was invited to be the eye of a nation, and he ignorantly, selfishly, or for whatever reason, turned down an opportunity of a lifetime.

Just be careful you don't miss your moment with God and destiny because God arranges for us to meet people. It is God who sets up circumstances, opportunities, and encounters in our lives. It is God who literally pulls people into our lives and, at times, takes others from our lives. However, for many people, because of personal and racial prejudices, indifference, and the feeling of intimidation, or for whatever reasons, they fail to recognize these theophoric encounters with God.

I call it 'theophoric" because it's like God walking into your life and ready to offer you an opportunity of a lifetime or open some great door of opportunity for you, but may you have God blocked out because of your lack of understanding of the moment.

Thank God Jacob did not miss his moment with God. After a wrestling match with the Angel of the Lord through the night, he said to the Angel, "you must be someone special. Would you please bless me before you leave"?

The Hobab Syndrome;

This is the problem that kept Hobab from yielding to the invitation of Moses. I nicknamed it the *'Hobab Syndrome'* because it is exhibited in many people's lives as what would have been a great door of opportunity comes their way.

Hobab saw in Moses and the Jews the weakness of a contingent of slaves coming out of Egypt and, for that matter, could not take them with any seriousness. In other words, "He couldn't see any potential in them besides their current status as poor and miserable slaves who had just escaped the Slave Master's whip."

Dear reader, like Hobab, did to Moses, some may have turned their backs on you on different occasions. Perhaps because upon sharing with them about the direction in which you felt the LORD was leading you, they perceived it as a joke.

At times people will just not take you seriously no matter what your vision, dreams, and aspirations are. After sharing your vision with them, they will say things like, "You said God spoke to you, and I was not there, and so you deal with it alone." I have met people who just don't take me seriously and to make matters worse, when I open my mouth to speak, my African ascent makes some to begin to look at me very funny as if to say what has this little African man to offer. Suppose you have ever been in that kind of situation before. In that case, it is alright because, with time, God will cause some of them to see your star in the East, and they are going to follow you into the safe habitations of your God-given destiny.

In conclusion, - yes, Moses and the children of Israel did not seem to have any potential when they ask Hobab for help. Yes, they were the children and grandchildren of slaves. Besides, they were scanty in number, compared to the heathen nations surrounding them. Also, it is no secret that they were weak both physically as individuals and corporately as a nation. Of course, from traveling the scourging wilderness, what would you expect other than physical weakness. However, what Hobab failed to see because he was spiritually short-sighted is hand of the almighty God that was with Moses and Israel's young nation. Hobab could not fathom the Omni-presence of the "All-sufficient God" with them in their infant stages as a nation.

Among the applicable life lessons that we can each learn and take away from Cain's life is that:

- *We need each other. As the saying goes, "No man is an Island."*
- *We should live for the sake of one another.*
- *We should care for one another because, of course, we are one another's keeper.*
- *As humans, we are all inter-connected and draw strength from each other's presence.*

This admonishment may seem contrary to modern-day conventional wisdom whereby selfishness and self-centeredness have become the order of the day. That's why more and more, we are seeing the influx of self-promotion, self-image, self-help, self-actualization, and self-worth -books, videos, movies, presentations, and resources flooding the market.

On the contrary, isn't it interesting to note that the central theme of the good news that Jesus preached was on self-denial instead of self-actualization?

Jesus said, ***"if any man will come after me, let him deny himself and take up his cross....".***

Taking up the cross of Christ represents bearing others' burdens and being sensitive to others' needs. Especially towards those who are not fortunate enough to possess the gifts, talents, and natural abilities you have been blessed with.

I have noticed that when many preach about Bible characters such as Cain and others who had apparent short-comings, they always stop at their sins, their short-comings, and the consequences they may have borne for their sins. However, I found out that God, on the other hand, does not stop at their short-comings and failures but instead continues to deal with them until their redemption is fulfilled.

Who would think that Cain of all people would ever make a come-back after orchestrating such an act of wickedness against his only brother? Moreover, he spoke back rudely to God upon being questioned about the whereabouts of his brother. Christ came to die for our pitfalls and shortfalls because of grace, and grace in itself is a redemption story. I can cite countless examples in the Bible of people who had disappointing beginnings in their life journey, but turned around and became Champions of godliness.

Among these examples are some like Moses, and Miriam, who had good intentions and also began well, but nearly ended up forfeiting all they had worked for because of their errors. However, God, in His abundance of love and grace, showed them mercy. In Moses's case, Satan even attempted to capitalize on his errors and, as basis to contend for the body of Moses; however, the Angel of the Lord rebuked Satan.

Others like Paul, Jacob, Peter, David, etc. did not start well and messed up really bad. Still, again like always, God brought great redemption their way, and they ended up becoming pillars of the faith in their day. Cain had a bad resume and a reputation that no other human being could challenge or contest. He was the first-ever murderer recorded in the entire history of humanity. No one can tell where Cain got the idea from -that another's life can be taken away from them.

God's warning to Cain before he killed his brother was, ***"If thou does well, will thou not be accepted; but if thou doesn't not well, sin is at your door and to you shall its pleasure be."***

I believe Cain's come back resulted from a change of heart. This is because people heading in the wrong direction usually don't turn their life around unless they have a strong reason to do so. He made a change of mind first, and then followed it by his action. According to the parable of the prodigal son as told by Jesus, ***"He said to himself even servants in my father's house have enough to eat and drink, so why should I be starving here in this deplorable situation. I will arise and go back to my father and say; you don't have to accept me as a son; just make me one of your servants" Luke 15:17-18.***

So, the redemptive story began with Cain himself. We got to know about it only after he had his first son and named him *Enoch*, or (Hanach) in Hebrew. Which means ***'now educated*** (**dedicated**).' After that, he built a city with the apparent goal to populate it with people, because why would one build a city if he or she wants to be by themselves. This is far from the Cain that the Bible described in the early chapters of the book of Genesis before he was driven into isolation in the land of Nod. His new identity is also far-fetched from Cain's old personality. Besides naming his son after he changed his mind, the story of Cain's redemption gets even more interesting when Cain built a city intending to welcome others to live together in harmony with him. Notice also that again, he named the city after his son Enoch to re-emphasize that he is a changed person. The Cain that left Eden was wicked and unwelcoming to others. However, the Cain that returned from isolation in the land of Nod was very accommodating to others. Even to the extent that he builds a habitation not just for himself but also to accommodate other people's needs.

> 1 Peter 2:10 says, *"We which in time past were not a people, but are now the people of God: which had not obtained mercy, but now have obtained mercy."*

The word *redemption* as used in the New Testament comes from the Greek ***"apolytrosis,"*** which means;

1. *A release effected by payment of ransom.*
2. *Liberation procured by the payment of a ransom.*

Therefore, no matter how bad it may seem, no one's

condition is beyond God's reach and redemptive power. This is because there is no price too high that God cannot pay. Neither is there any condition too hopeless that God cannot penetrate with His love for His creation to purchase their redemption?

Adam and Eve's Redemption

Notice also that God's redemption plan in Eden did not end with Cain. It reached out far beyond Cain. It was extended to his parents Adam and Eve, who most probably may have passed the age of bearing children because they may be too old in age at the time.

We, however, read from the last but one verse of Genesis Chapter four (Gen. 4;25), that;

> [25] ***Adam made love to his wife <u>again</u>, and she gave birth to a son and named him Seth,[h] saying, "God has granted me another child in place of Abel since Cain killed him."***
> [26] ***Seth also had a son, and he named him Enos. At that time, people began to call on[i] the name of the LORD.***

In other words, God's redemptive plan was not only extended to Cain in his restoration from a lonely life. Still, it was also extended to his parents Adam and Eve, who had lost their son Abel due to Cain's wickedness. God brought redemption to Adam and Eve, so their bodies will be naturally revitalized or quickened for them to have another son in place of Abel, whom Cain killed. Notice that using the word *'again'* is essential in the above text because it implies they were over and done with childbearing. Still, God had to reverse that natural order to allow their bodies to produce seed in replacement for the son they lost. If you think I am making this up, see for yourself what the Bible specifically said about this;

> ***"Adam made love to his wife again, and she gave birth to a son and named him Seth,[h] saying, "God has granted me another child in place of Abel since Cain killed him."***.

The birth of Seth, therefore, was a redemption story. Seth was born for the sole purpose of replacing the son that was lost through the murder of Abel. This is nothing short of a beautiful story of God's redemption that goes far beyond Cain, the rebel. It reaches unto his aged parents who had left childbearing perhaps decades before their unexpected third and last son Seth was born. This third and final child by Adam and Eve was born after the sixth generation of Cain's descendants. We are told that Cain had Enoch (2nd generation). Enoch also had Irad (3rd generation). Irad begot Mehujael (4th generation), Mehujael begot Methushael (5th generation), and Methushael begot Lamech (6th generation), which is the sixth generations from Cain. It was also before Cain's parents unexpectedly had Seth. Genesis 5;3 also confirms that Seth was born to Adam and Eve when Adam was at an old age of 130.

> **Gen. 5:3 *"When Adam had lived 130 years, he had a son in his own likeness, in his own image; and he named him Seth."***

This indeed is a redemption story like no other that I have come across in the Bible. Since God did the same for Abraham and Sarah many years after, why doubt that God did it for Adam and Eve, even generations before Abraham and Sarah. If you believe Abraham and Sarah's story, then you've got to believe Adam and Eve's story as well because it is the same good God working through both couples. What the Lord has done before, He will undoubtedly do it again. This is because, with God, all things are possible. He also is the same yesterday, today, and will forever be the same. While things may change with time, God never changes.

Cain's name went down in records as the first human ever to commit murder in the history of all humanity. However, his name also went down in record as the first man ever whose descendant will defy death. This descendant of Cain was Enoch by name.

The Bible says about Cain's direct descendant by name Enoch in **Gen 5:24...**

> ***"And Enoch walked with God: and he was not; for God took him."***

This is a direct descendant of Cain, who found so much favor before the Lord such that God allowed him to depart the earth without experiencing death. Isn't that awesome that God would do such a marvelous thing for a descendant of Cain.?

That, however, did not mark the end of the redemption story. Another direct descendant of Cain, by name Methuselah, was also so highly favored by God that he lived longer than any mortal being in the entire history of humanity. In **Genesis 5:27**, we are told;

> ***And all the days of Methuselah were nine hundred † sixty and nine (969 years): and he died.***

Methuselah's life is talked about as much as any man that ever lived, other than Jesus Christ. The reason being that he lived longer than any other man.

Rabbi Yacov Rambsell, in his book "Yeshua; The Name of Jesus Revealed in Code in the Old Testament," noted that according to Jewish tradition, Methuselah died seven days before the era of the great flood of Noah. This was the time that God poured out His judgment upon a sinful and rebellious world. Could it be that New Testament believers would be removed (resurrected) one week (seven years) before the nations' judgment?

It is also worth noting that Methuselah witnessed the preaching of Noah. However, he knew by the meaning of his name that he would be gone before the flood came. His name has different meanings. One is "when he is gone, then it shall happen." What shall happen? Most probably the impending judgment of God that was preached by Noah.

According to Jude 14-15, Enoch also spoke about the same impending judgment of God.

Jude 14-15

> ***"And Enoch also, the seventh from Adam, prophesied of these, saying, Behold, the***

> ***Lord cometh with ten thousands of his saints, To execute judgment upon all, and to convince all that are ungodly among them of all their ungodly deeds which they have ungodly committed, and of all their hard speeches which ungodly sinners have spoken against him"***

Unlike Methuselah, whose meaning of his name suggests that he was gone from the face of the earth by the time of Noah's flood, God saw it fit to translate Enoch before the flood of Noah came. This, in a way, suggest that before God pours out His wrath upon the ungodly world of today, He will also translate (rapture) those believers in that day who, like Enoch, walked with Jesus Christ. This is because the reason why Enoch was translated was that his ways pleased God, and so shall it be for them whose ways please God.

The Hebrew word *'toshiyah'* is; "Salvation by God through a man." As a result, God promised to wrought salvation to Noah and his family upon their entrance into the ark. Therefore, for all who will give heed to the gospel of Jesus Christ and will enter the ark of God, God will bring salvation to them through a man named Jesus Christ, the Savior of the world.

If God will bend over and show all these favors to Cain and his direct descendants, then why can't He do the same for you? Only God knows. If so, be that the direct descendants of Cain were so blessed of the Lord. There is undoubtedly a redemption story behind every failure. There is a redemption story behind every disappointment.

There is a redemption story as well behind every shortfall in life. There is a redemption story behind every misfortune that you may go through. Therefore, I say to you today that there is a redemption story behind whatever negativities, adversities, disappointments, and struggles that you may be going through in your life at the moment. If only you learn the lessons that come with it, your experience will be a blessing to others who may encounter the same or similar circumstances in their lives. Why don't you make a U-turn like Cain did and turn it all over to God the Maker and Creator of your being? I challenge you that you will never regret and never be the same if you do so. That reminds me of the popular hymn, "*Just as I Am*," written by Charlotte Elliott in 1835. It was noted that the final verse of the song was taken from Elliott's hours of sorrow.

John Brownlie vividly described the story behind the hymn in his book *"The Hymns and Hymn Writers of the Church Hymnary."* According to Charlotte Elliott's brother, the Rev. H. V. Elliott, she planned to hold a charity bazaar designed to give, at a nominal cost, a high education to the daughters of clergymen supported by St Mary Church.

The night before the bazaar, she was kept wakeful by distressing thoughts of her apparent uselessness. These thoughts passed by a transition easily to imagine into a spiritual conflict until she questioned the reality of her whole spiritual life. She also wondered whether it was anything better after all than an illusion of the emotions -an illusion ready to be sorrowfully dispelled. The next day, the busy day of the bazaar, she lay upon her sofa in that most pleasant boudoir set apart for her in Westfield Lodge, ever a lovely resort to her friends. The troubles of the night came back upon her with such force that she felt they must be met and conquered in the grace of God. She gathered up in her soul the great certainties, not of her emotions, but of her salvation - her Lord, His power, His promise. And taking pen and paper from the table, she deliberately set down in writing, for her own comfort, "the formulae of her faith." Hers was a heart that always tended to express its depths in verse. So in verse, she restated to herself the gospel of pardon, peace, and heaven. Probably without difficulty or long pause, wrote the hymn. Getting comfort by thus definitely recollecting the eternity of the Rock beneath her feet. There, then, always, not only for some past moments but even now she felt accepted in the Beloved.

Just as I am, without one plea
But that Thy Blood was shed for me,
And that Thou bidd'st me come to Thee,
O Lamb of God, I come, I come

Just as I am, poor, wretched, blind,
Sight, riches, healing of the mind,
Yea, all I need, in Thee to find,
O Lamb of God, I come, I come

Just as I am, Thou wilt receive,
Wilt welcome, pardon, cleanse, relieve;
Because Thy promise I believe,
O Lamb of God, I come, I come.

Just as I am, Thy love unknown
Has broken every barrier down
Now to be Thine, yea, Thine alone,
O Lamb of God, I come, I come.

No matter what you are going through at this moment, just keep the battle on. Don't sell out and don't carve in because your redemption draws near. According to Luke 21;28, when these things begin to come to pass, then look up and lift up your heads, for your redemption draws nigh.

APPENDIX 1

AUDIO TAPES BY THE AUTHOR

Tried, Tested and Proven

There are 3 phases to freedom. Bondage, Deliverance and Change in Mindset. Deliverance is not the same thing as Freedom because while deliverance is instantaneous, freedom is a process. Strikingly and interestingly, the Nation of Israel, Our Lord Jesus Christ, as well as every New Testament Believer, started their journey of faith from Egypt (Bondage).

- We all have to go through our first body of water (Red Sea)
- We all have to go through our share of trials & temptations (Wilderness)
- We all have to cross our second body of water (Jordan)
- But not all will be able to get to the promise land of Canaan (Freedom)

Managing Your God-giving Resources

This is a timely message of accountability for every Believer. God's prime purpose for creating man, according to the book of Genesis was to find a Manager for all His creation. Hence God will first test our trustworthiness before He entrust anything into our care. This is because to him the much is given, much shall be required, the bible says.

Kingdom Worship: The Universal Symphony of Effectual Praise

This 3 series tape will leave you amused and enlightened but definitely not bored. It is an in depth exposition of Psalm 149 and reveals how true worship should be in the sanctuary of our God based on the meaning of the common word Hallelujah. (Halal Yah)

Redeeming The Time

Have you ever thought of the fact that God does not live in time but created time for man to live in.? Time, is the most precious commodity that we have as humans. While we may have different ethnic backgrounds, may differ in knowledge, wealth, education etc., we are all given the same amount of time within each day. Therefore, what you end up becoming, is largely dependent on how you use your time. Time is too precious to waste so make sure you don't let it slip out of your hands unawares.

The Blood and Fire

A timeless message of rebellion, redemption and the God who is always compassionate towards his creation. This book reveals the true meaning of Pentecost and the ingredients without which Pentecost would have been a meaningless spiritual experience.

Don't Waste Your Suffering

Human suffering is a subject that has always baffled the minds and understanding of many. As humans, we will not understand it all but it is essential that we come to terms with suffering. God always have an agenda and a behind the scene plan for every suffering that we go through.

It's A Love Affair

True intimacy with God is a love affair. It is the kind of relationship that can only be experienced by the two who are in love with each other. Until we begin to see our relationship with God as such, we will be distance from the true lover of our soul.

Who is Sitting At Your Table

At the table set for Jesus in the house of Mary of Bethany, there were many others including Jesus. However, while some were skeptics whose only reason for being at the table was to see for themselves that indeed Lazarus had been raised from the dead by Jesus, there were however, others who truly believed in Jesus as the Son of God. Who is sitting at the head of the table of your life?.

Printed in the United States
By Bookmasters